FROM ECONOMIC MAN TO ECONOMIC SYSTEM

All but one of the essays in this volume discuss topics involving human behavior and the institutions of capitalism. The exception discusses interdisciplinary work and, particularly, the differences between the ways that biology and economics treat competition. The essays are written so as to be accessible to students of all disciplines and to all other persons interested in capitalism and in economic behavior. They are not text-like treatments, but they do offer useful supplementary readings of an unusual sort for courses in business, economics, and law in matters relating to human behavior, capitalism, ownership, markets, and firms.

Harold Demsetz is Arthur Anderson UCLA Alumni Emeritus Professor of Business Economics at the University of California, Los Angeles, where he has taught since 1971 and where he directed UCLA's business economics program. He earned a Ph.D. from Northwestern University in 1959. Counted among the world's 100 most eminent economists in Mark Blaug's book *Great Economists Since Keynes*, Professor Demsetz also holds honorary doctorates from Northwestern University and Francisco Marraquin University. His published work was recently ranked as among the top ten most frequently cited bodies of works by an economist. *Who's Who in America* and *Who's Who in Economics*, among other directories, include his biography.

A Fellow of the American Academy of Arts and Sciences and past president of the Western Economics Association International, Professor Demsetz has also served as Director of the Mont Pelerin Society and of the International Society for New Institutional Economics. He has been a senior editor of the *Supreme Court Economic Review*, a founding member of the American Society of Law and Economics, and a member of the advisory boards of the *International Journal of Economics and Business* and the *Journal of Corporate Finance*.

Professor Demsetz's research is focused on property rights, the business firm, and problems in monopoly, competition, and antitrust. He is the author of numerous professional articles, four books, and three published monographs of honorary lectures. His most recent book, *The Economics of the Business Firm: Seven Critical Commentaries* (Cambridge University Press, 1995), has been translated into Chinese, French, and Spanish.

FROM ECONOMIC MAN TO ECONOMIC SYSTEM

Essays on Human Behavior and the Institutions of Capitalism

HAROLD DEMSETZ

University of California, Los Angeles

CAMBRIDGE
UNIVERSITY PRESS

32 Avenue of the Americas, New York NY 10013-2473, USA

Cambridge University Press is part of the University of Cambridge.

It furthers the University's mission by disseminating knowledge in the pursuit of education, learning and research at the highest international levels of excellence.

www.cambridge.org
Information on this title: www.cambridge.org/9780521509978

First published 2008

A catalogue record for this publication is available from the British Library

Library of Congress Cataloguing in Publication data

Demsetz, Harold, 1930–
From economic man to economic system : essays on human behavior and the institutions of capitalism / Harold Demsetz.
p. cm.
Includes bibliographical references and index.
ISBN 978-0-521-50997-8 (hardback)
1. Capitalism. 2. Economic man. I. Title.
HB501.D424   2008
330.12′2 – dc22   2008008955

ISBN 978-0-521-50997-8 Hardback

Future reading for
Esther, Richard, Aaron, Helen, Emily, Natalie, and Ben

CONTENTS

Contents

INTRODUCTION: ABOUT THESE ESSAYS

THE LAST TWO CENTURIES HAVE REVEALED AN UPWARD, BUT unsteady, trend of capitalism in many portions of the world. And, during the same interval of time, there has beeen an upward trend in the reputation of the discipline of economics. In one sense, these are strongly related, since puzzlement about the economic system that we now call capitalism motivated much of the mainline work done by economists during this interval. However, in another sense, the two happenings are, or have become, unrelated, since much economic theory describes human behavior and production opportunies in ways that are not specific to a type of economic system. Thus, the first law of demand – the negative relationship between the quantity of a good acquired by a person and the cost (or, in capitalism, the price) of acquiring the good – is testably operative in every type of economic system. Similarly, the relationship between the unit cost of producing a good, measured in terms of amount of resources committed to its production, and the total number of units of the good produced is a question of technology, not of economic system.

The main difference between economic systems is in regard to the constraints that are applied to human behavior. The fact is that students of economics learn much about universally applicable propositions and little about the institutions that define applicable constraints. The primary reason for this is that those who created much of economic theory simply *presumed* they were writing about an economy based on private ownership of resources; they further presumed that those who would learn what they had written would possess an understanding of a private ownership system. Each of the essays in this volume has its own purpose, but the nature and role of the institutions of capitalism are discussed in many of them.

I intend these essays for a broad audience, but I especially hope to reach students and teachers of economics and the law. I make little use of technical jargon or formal models, so these essays are accessible even to people who are not specialized to these disciplines or even any other discipline. All the essays, save one, fit the themes implied by this book's title. The last essay, which discusses interdisciplinary work, is an exception to this claim. Its presence in this volume is due mainly to the presence of three other essays, *Rescuing Economic Man from Selfish Gene Theory*, *The Late Arrival of Capitalism*, and *Economic Man's Escape from Malthus's Population Trap*, all of which in greater or lesser degree involve disciplines other than economics.

I have touched on some of the topics covered here in other papers I have written, but these earlier appearances have been light and incidental in comparison to the treatments given them in this volume, and many topics discussed here have not had an earlier appearance. One exception to this is the essay *Firms and Households as Substitutes*. It is essentially a revision of a few pages contained in my *The Economics of the Business Firm* (1995). It is included here for two reasons – to make more clear some of what I had written earlier and to round out and complete the line of reasoning I use in the essay *Reinterpreting the Externality Problem*; these two essays, taken together, give a full explanation of my dissatisfaction with the way "transaction cost economics" has been used in the study of economic organization.

The essays progress from discussions of individual behavior to discussions of economic institutions, but they are meant to stand alone. The writng of each essay has its own starting point. A few examples explain what I mean. The first essay, "Where Economic Man Dwells," responds to frequently expressed concerns of students about the emphasis given in economics to self interested behavior. The essay on "Reinterpreting the Externality Problem" reflects the doubts I have accumulated as I attempted to explain R. H. Coase's (1960) notable discussion of the problem of social cost to students. The essay "Rescuing Economic Man from Selfish Gene Theory" springs from a reading of Dawkins interesting work on *The Selfish Gene* (1976) and from my realization that the *gene* as *the* seeker of self-interest leaves little room for the *person*. The essay on *The Late Arrival of Capitalism* emerges partly from a reading of *Guns, Germs, and Steel* (1997) by Jared Diamond. Diamond's book brought a bevy of facts to my attention, some of which are used in this essay to resolve a phenomenon about which I had been puzzling. Why did mankind fail to develop the institutions of capitalism during the first ninety-nine percent of known human existence? In answering this question, I was brought to an explanation for the rise of capitalism. Diamond's explanation of the success of Western civilization seems inadequate because it is mostly descriptive of innovational change and lacking in a theory by which to tie these changes into an explanation of Western progress.

The approach of these essays is in the spirit of positive economics, but I am sure that my normative preferences rise to the surface here and there. I hope this has not occured often. As with the other claims I have made, there is an exception. The essay "Protecting You from Yourself" is expressly normative; and justifiably so because it deals with ideas of writers such as Thorstein Veblen, John K. Galbraith, and Robert H. Frank that are quite normative.

[3]

Introduction: About These Essays

Early in my writing of these essays, I thought about giving this volume the title *Open for Discussion*. This describes my hope in writing these essays but it does not describe this volume's contents, so I chose instead to call it *From Economic Man to Economic System*. However, please join the discussion.

ON SELF-INTEREST

The doctrine of self-interest properly understood does not inspire great sacrifices, but every day it prompts some small ones; by itself it cannot make a man virtuous, but its discipline shapes a lot of orderly, temperate, moderate, careful, and self controlled citizens. If it does not lead to virtue, it establishes habits which unconsciously turn it that way.

Providence did not make mankind entirely free or completely enslaved. Providence has, in truth, drawn a predestined circle around each man beyond which he cannot pass; but within those vast limits man is strong and free, and so are peoples.

(Alexis de Tocqueville)

1 WHERE ECONOMIC MAN DWELLS[1]

L ET ME INTRODUCE YOU TO ECONOMIC MAN. BUT, WAIT, YOU
know him already. He is Scrooge before being reformed by
ghosts of past and future times. He is the landlord in Puccini's *La
Boheme*, who has the audacity to ask his poor, unemployed, and
fun-seeking artist tenants for the rent due him. He is the banker
who pressures a destitute widow to make the due mortgage payment. He is Veblen's predatory businessman of the 1890s, skilled
at calculating and at pressuring rivals into submission. He thinks
only of himself and, mainly, only of his wealth. He is ridiculed
by critics who see him as a caricature of a real person, and who,
therefore, drum him out of the human species by reclassifying
him as *Homo economicus*. Yet, he is present within each of us and,
more important for these essays, he is alive and well in economics.
In this essay, I consider why this is so. First, however, I note the
following three points:

(1) The task of understanding market processes is different from
that of understanding a human being and even from that of understanding issues that are not ordinarily resolved through market
processes. Except with respect to human intelligence, economics
does not describe a person in a way that might serve the needs

---

[1] This essay develops an idea that I set forth in my Presidential Address before the Western
Economic Society in 1996 (published 1997).

of biologists, sociologists, and philosophers. It did not, until fairly recently, give much thought to the workings of institutions other than markets. I make this clear even though I suspect that the economic analysis of the marketplace has much to offer in these regards.

Other social sciences are focused on problems that differ in various degrees from problems of the marketplace, and, appropriately enough, they view a person somewhat differently from the way economists do. Each of these different perceptions about human behavior are to be thought of as tools that serve specific purposes, not as complete, accurate descriptions of people. Failure to recognize this has been a major source of confusion.

(2) Although self-interest means serving one's own wants, it does not specify these wants. For reasons given below, this essay, for the most part, will assume that these wants do not include the well-being of others; the assumption is not an imperative of the economic model of human behavior but it allows this essay to deal with the caricature of economic man created by the model's critics.

There is bias in this caricature. Consider again the persons depicted in Puccini's opera. The landlord is cast as a dolt and narrow-minded seeker of rent; no matter that he has invested considerable sums in providing living spaces to those in need of them. His artist-tenants, on the other hand, are viewed as kind, fun-loving pleasure seekers. They acquire such pleasures by delaying payments of the rent due the landlord, which is narrow-mindedly seeking to use the funds of someone else, and by succeeding in bilking an elderly, past lover of coquettish Musseta. Now, I ask you, which of these two classes of characters is the more narrow-mindedly self-seeking? They both seek their self-interests. The difference between them is in the methods employed. The landlord supplies living space and offers contractual arrangements to use this space, expecting thereby to receive funds from tenants. The elderly lover buys lunch for others out of past remembrances of romance and present hopes of renewing this romance. The artists, on the other hand, pursue self-interests in duplicitous ways, delaying performance on the rental agreement that provides them with living space and deceiving an elderly seeker of romantic engagement. Critics of economic man generally visualize the landlord-type as the only person who fits the caricature they have fashioned.

(3) Human behavior does reflect concern for others. We know this from life within the family, interactions within the workplace and military platoon, and so on. Conscious cooperation with and personal feelings toward others are important in these areas of human activity.[2] Yet, it is precisely the narrower interpretation of human behavior, as motivated by concern for one's own wants, that makes the economic model of behavior so useful in the study of activity in the marketplace. And it is the marketplace that is the arena of behavior most relevant to what, historically, has been the central problem of economics. This essay explains why this is so.

I

Economic man remains alive in economics because he is very helpful to the resolution of what arguably is the most important puzzle economists faced during the first 150 years during which their discipline matured into a social science. This puzzle has been aptly described in contemporary times by F. A. Hayek (1988) as that of "spontaneous order": "spontaneous" because no person or group of persons, and no institution, determines how resources will be allocated in the liberal economy; a "puzzle" because, despite the absence of managed, conscious control there seems to emerge a "sensible" allocation of resources.

---

[2] Indeed, my colleague Armen Alchian and I cooperated in writing an article (1972) that stressed the importance of team production to the organization of the firm.

This puzzle not only shaped the discipline of economics, it also distinguished economics from the other social sciences. It plays no important role in other social sciences, not in anthropology, political science, or sociology, and, if these be social sciences, not in psychology and neuroscience. Not even in biology.

The model of human behavior used in economics is a tool applied to gain an understanding of how the decentralization puzzle is resolved, and, like any tool, it is specialized to its primary task. It emphasizes some aspects of human behavior while repressing others. Concern about one's own wants is emphasized; concern for the wants of others is slighted. Critics of economic man often express a preference for a model of human behavior that is more broadly conceived, one that incorporates all, or most, aspects of human behavior; it would meld concern for one's own wants with concern for the wants of others. No consensus has yet emerged about the formal nature of such a model, but there is no necessary advantage to a comprehensive model of human behavior. A tool fashioned to hammer nails is not made more useful by attaching a screwdriver to it. Multiple models of human behavior, each specialized to be useful in the examination of different important problems, may be more successful in solving different types of problems, although, human curiosity being what it is, there will remain the problem of a unified theory of human behavior. Like the quest for a unified theory of physical-chemical properties, a unified theory of human behavior may be a long time in coming. Meanwhile, solutions to particular types of human behavioral problems may be most expeditiously obtained through the use of specialized models of human behavior.

Extensive decentralization, characterized by independently acting private owners of resources, describes the core of the spontaneous order problem. The marketplace, in turn, is the dominant arena in which independently acting persons interact with each other in deciding how the resources they own are to be used. The virtue of the economic model of man is that it is well suited to the task of exploring behavior in this arena, *whether this is located in a solidly capitalistic economy or in a solidly socialistic economy.*

II

Conditions in the marketplace differ from those within the family, neighborhood, and political bureaucracy. They even differ from those that exist within the business firm, since people within the firm, because of their long-term association with, and dependency on, each other, cease to act in full neglect of each other. Perhaps this is why mainstream economists writing during the neoclassical period of their discipline gave little attention to what goes on inside the business firm.

Personalized interactions, borne of durable associations, also characterize dealings between family members, neighbors, and fellow bureaucrats. Emotionalizing and strategizing are much more likely in these institutional settings than in the marketplace. The setting that is consistent with the spontaneous order problem is that in which people make their decisions independently, meaning that their decisions are not affected by knowledge of or concern for how they might affect others. That setting is not the home. It is not the neighborhood. It is not the firm. It is, for reasons to be given, the marketplace.

Exchange in the marketplace is treated as exchange between persons who are essentially unknown to each other. Indeed, in the highly organized marketplace, people, buyers and sellers, do not face each other. They face prices. In the economic conception of the highly organized marketplace, there is no personalized interaction between buyer and seller; each simply acts independently in responding to an impersonally determined market price, making his or her decisions on the basis of this price and his or her own wants. Interactions between people within home and workplace are laden with personalized knowledge of those involved. Because of this, they imply conscious interaction between knowing people, not the independent decision making that is central to a meaningful notion of extreme decentralization. Decisions within home and workplace, therefore, are less useful in the task of unraveling the puzzle of *spontaneously* produced order. In the setting of the highly organized marketplace, in contrast, there is no other person about whom a buyer or seller has personal knowledge or personal regard. Think of the offer to purchase or sell shares of stock on an organized exchange.

Markets in a real economy often differ somewhat from the economic conception of a highly organized market. They sometimes involve familiarity between people, but the degree of familiarity is less than that which would normally exist within households and firms. Owners and customers of local grocery stores, dry-cleaning establishments, and other such businesses are acquainted. So are doctors and patients, and so on. Frequent interaction between the same people makes for some familiarity and perhaps for more personalized concern. So, yes, the highly organized market gives a somewhat distorted view of the "neighborhood" setting, but the neighborhood setting is not that of the spontaneous order puzzle. Moreover, by how much is the local setting distorted by the economic model of human behavior? Do sympathetic feelings between buyer and seller have a large influence on decisions involved in neighborhood shopping? Have you offered the local grocer more for his goods than the price he posts or asks, or do you search among competing neighborhood grocers for best values? Do you offer more if the grocer is on the verge of bankruptcy? How much more, how often, and for how long? Personalization of exchange at the local level mostly involves cheery greetings and casual inquiries about how well things are going. Seldom do they involve significant deviation from self-interested calculation of the sort that is clearly present in the highly organized market. Although economists have not ignored localized arenas of human behavior, I have yet to see an empirical study that is made more powerful because it substitutes dealings between "Sam the tailor" and "Jane the successful busi-nesswoman" for dealings between persons who are strangers.[3]

The German buyer of American wheat does not know, and does not care to know, who produced the wheat. He has no desire to pay more than the market price for wheat, and those who supply wheat have no desire to ask a price lower than is available on the market. If drought conditions reduce the supply of wheat, raising the price per bushel, do farmers, in sympathy for buyers of wheat, offer to sell a bushel for less than it can fetch in the market? If plentiful rain increases the supply of wheat, thereby decreasing its price, do buyers, in sympathy for farmers, offer more per bushel than the market asks them to pay?

My point is by now quite obvious. In coming to an understanding of spontaneous order there is considerable methodological useful-ness in minimizing the attention one gives to emotionalism and concern for others. However, economic man's usefulness is not just a matter of methodology. He is useful in other respects. We observe two codes of behavior in dealings between people. In commercial dealings "business is business," meaning that acceptable behav-ior is honest and reliable, not loving, hating, or sympathizing. In dealings within family and community, where continuing personal association is important, behavior is expected to exhibit care, char-ity, and sympathy. A desire, expressed by many persons of good will, to make dealings in the marketplace more like those between neighbors and between family members, simply fails to compre-hend the impossibility of this if good will is meted out mainly to those with whom one is familiar. Suppose that buyer and seller do personally meet while engaging in a transaction. If the buyer offers a price higher than is needed to conclude the transaction,

---

[3] I refer to normal economic conditions here, not interactions that might follow a devas-tating earthquake or some other catastrophe. Behavior does become different, but only very temporarily, in such special settings, but these are inappropriate to the study of spontaneous order.

doing so in an act of good will toward the seller, then he will make members of his family worse off for bringing less "bacon" home than he could have secured. Similarly, for the seller's family if the seller should offer to sell for less than he could have secured from the buyer. If closeness of association correlates with sympathetic feelings, buyer and seller will ignore each other's interest and tend instead to their own and their family's interest. On a deeper level, this behavior may be explainable in terms of genes that selfishly seek their own survival (although, of course, this presumes that persons on other sides of the exchange are not close relatives).

The view I have just presented confronts the caricature used by critics of the economic model, but let us back away from the highly organized markets that I have discussed in order to focus on this caricature. As noted early in this essay, to seek one's self-interest is not to describe what adds to or subtracts from a feeling of well-being. We know that people who engage in exchange across highly organized markets, and who generally do so without sympathetic feelings for reasons given above, also make contributions to causes that they think worthwhile but that do not directly add to, and generally subtract from, their wealth. When such contributions are made voluntarily, they are made to recipients known to, or believed to, serve these causes, so, in a sense, people are not dealing with prices or completely unknown persons. Such knowledge can also come through market processes. Many people invest in funds and stocks that specialize in companies that do not produce products thought to be damaging to the environment or to the health of those who use them.

Once knowledge of this kind is demanded, it will be supplied through markets; the exchange, then, is not between complete strangers. Such knowledge implies a reduction in the degree of independence between those who own resources. In effect, an investor offers funds *if* the recipient continues to produce goods that do not harm environment or health. There is realism in this, but focusing on this behavior is a cumbersome way to resolve the spontaneous order problem; "decentralization," after all, means independent decision making by those who do not know each other. Economists have been intensely interested in understanding how order emerges from such independence. Order that emerges from dependent interaction seems too uninteresting; an employer tells an employee what to do and, generally, it gets done. However, viewed on a scale that could be described as central planning, dependent interaction presents a serious and complicated puzzle, one that we are not close to resolving.

III

Interaction between strangers – even we recognize this as an extreme condition of markets – often is a close approximation to reality. This closeness comes from the fact that specialization of economic activity is an important source of productivity for many human activities, and especially for market-relevant activities. Specialization has several meanings. Here, it means production of large quantities of a single good (or a few goods) by a comparatively small number of people, this production to be sold to large numbers of persons (consumers) who do not themselves engage in production of the good. Specialization stands in opposition to self-sufficiency. Dealing with large numbers of buyers makes it impractical to establish personalized relationships between producer and consumers. People seeking automobiles would find their personal involvement in producing an automobile wasteful of their time and efforts. They prefer instead to purchase it at lower cost (or higher quality) from someone, from a firm, that specializes in manufacturing and selling automobiles. The purchaser cannot maintain a highly personalized relationship with the specialists who have produced the plastic, steel, cloth, rubber, wire, and glass that go into the product, nor can he or she know those who assemble, check, and transport the vehicle. Even the specialists whose work is used to produce automobiles, by virtue of being employed in their separate and different specialties, are generally strangers to each other. Nor can the owners and managers of the firm that specializes in automobile production personally know the thousands of persons who purchase the firm's product. The marketplace characterized by dealings between near-strangers is an imperative of the fact that specialization, for many activities, is highly productive. This productivity cannot be realized if exchange is to take place only between people who are very familiar with (and sympathetic toward) each other.

Contemporary developed economies extensively rely on specialization, but we need not look to contemporary times to appreciate the degree to which production is characterized by specialized activity. C. C. Allen (1929), in his study of economic development in England around the year 1860, reports of the small arms industry:

> The master gun-maker – the entrepreneur – seldom possessed a factory or workshop.... Usually he owned merely a warehouse in the gun quarter [of Birmingham], and his function was to acquire semi-finished parts and to give these out to specialized craftsmen, who undertook the assembly and finishing of the gun. He purchased materials from the barrel-makers, lock-makers, sight-stampers, trigger-makers, ramrod-forgers, gun-furniture makers, and, if he were engaged in the military branch, from bayonet-forgers.... Once the parts had been purchased ... the next task was to hand them out to a long succession of "setters-up," each of whom performed a specific operation in connection with the assembly and finishing of the gun. To name only a few, there were those who prepared the front sight and lump end of the barrels; the jiggers, who attended to the breech end; the stockers, who let in the barrel and lock and shaped the stock; the barrel-strippers, who prepared the gun for rifling and proof; the hardeners, polishers, borers and riflers, engravers, browners, and finally the lock-freers, who adjusted the working parts. (pp. 116–17)

The description just quoted applies to the activities of specialists who are involved in the production of just one type of final product. Of course, there also is specialization across products. Gun makers do not make breakfast cereals, home builders do not grow corn, and so on.

Dispositions of people, probably acquired during primitive times, make them suspicious of strangers and reluctant to deal with them, preferring instead to deal with family and clan members. This might be explained in biological terms by theories based on gene survival, but it also might be explained in economic terms by the lower monitoring and disciplining costs that come with close, continuing association within the family and clan. The give-and-take of people in a small group setting and the knowledge they possess about each other make members of such groups more reliable deliverers of reciprocal favors, gifts, and payments, but the small group dealing within its own boundaries cannot realize the considerable gains that can be secured from scale-favoring specialization. These gains are greatest if a good is produced in very large quantities and sold to large numbers of buyers. If a society is to realize these gains it must create conditions that make exchange between strangers tolerably reliable. Contract law and civility toward strangers provide this reliability. Thus, potential gains from specialization bring forth not only markets and dealings between strangers, but also the laws, customs, and cultures that reduce suspicions of and antagonistic actions toward strangers. It is not so much the result of persuasion by moralists, intellectuals, and religious leaders that is the source of civil society as it is the productivity gain offered by scale-favoring specialization.

Civil dealings make dealings with strangers more reliable because, in fact, they introduce a degree of personalization into the market. If stranger deals with stranger, why not take advantage of the transaction by not holding up your end of the exchange? Those who would behave this way must become (probabilistically) identifiable and/or financially committed. There are a variety of ways of accomplishing this: requiring information on past performance, up-front commitments of funds to a forthcoming transaction, and simultaneity in meeting exchange obligations, for example. Protections against fraud offered by credit cards are another example. These arrangements function as substitutes for the reliability in dealings found within a small group of closely associated persons. All these arrangements are inconsistent with a strictly defined notion that markets are arenas in which strangers deal with strangers, even though they can be applied in ways that are compatible with this notion. The market itself, say the New York Stock Exchange, requires an up-front commitment of funds and threatens exposure of poor performance, but it does not make those doing the transacting knowledgeable about each other's identities or even about each other's performance in similar dealings. The "price" of admission to the market is acceptance of the market's trading requirements. Institutional mechanisms are put into place to make people comfortable in dealing with strangers. It is true that these mechanisms distinguish people, particularly by separating those who do qualify to trade from those who do not. A degree of personalization, then, is present in exchange activities, but it is not a great deal of personalization, nor is it of a sort that creates charitable or angry feelings between those on the opposite side of an exchange. In these respects, the marketplace does service dealings between persons who are emotionally unconnected.

Neoclassical economics, moreover, did not concern itself with disagreements about terms of trade, failure to perform on transactions, or defective dealings in markets. It sought to understand resource allocation if prices *actually do* inform decisions about available opportunities and if these opportunities *really are* realized. To allow for disagreements and failures to perform would require not price guidance but absence of, or defective, price guidance.

IV

To conclude this essay, I note that, though I think the marketplace is a valuable institution through which to allocate resources, the essay itself is not driven by moral judgment about the marketplace. My argument is simply that human behavior, good and bad, is well explained by modeling it as pursuing narrowly defined "own" wants when dealing with interactions across markets; "own" wants, instead of "sympathetic" wants, call the tune because of the considerable gains in productivity that are realized through the use of scale-favoring production techniques. None of this implies that the goods produced and exchanged are justifiable in moral terms; they simply are *wanted* goods. When exchange takes place, people get more of what they want, not necessarily more of what is good or bad for society or good or bad for them. The morality of relying on the marketplace (or on the polling place) depends in large part on the moral value that we attach to actions taken freely and interactions engaged in voluntarily.

Something like moral quality is misleadingly suggested by the vocabulary used to describe the behavior of economic man. He seeks to maximize *utility, self-interest,* or *well-being.* The spontaneous order puzzle asks how a *sensible* allocation of resources emerges from a setting in which conscious coordination and central planning are absent. All these words suggest a beneficial outcome for the individual and a lack of concern for the larger society, but all the economic model really assumes is that people know and act on what they *want.* What they want is not necessarily good for them or for others. The "sensible" allocation of resources is not to be interpreted to mean socially, personally, or morally correct or incorrect. It means only (1) that each person's wants are satisfied to the degree that he or she is willing to pay the cost incurred to service these wants and (2) that markets clear; which is to say that all that is wanted is supplied and all that is supplied is wanted (and acquired). These outcomes are not unimportant, and they are not irrelevant to morally evaluating behavior in the marketplace. The economic model that deduces them contributes importantly to our understanding of the marketplace. However, this triumph of the mind does not itself sustain judgments about the moral quality of dealings in the marketplace. Capitalism and markets are not the equivalent of a church or a moral code, or a school for terrorists.

They function on the basis of good-faith dealings with others, not with what people do or do not want. What you want has its origins elsewhere. If natural selection has given rise to the favoring of self and one's own over others and their own, well, that is a product of natural selection and of the failure of preachers and moralists to alter very much that which natural selection has produced. Such discrimination, if it is in fact inbred in most people, will become most evident in highly organized markets, not because they are markets, but because they are forums where strangers deal with each other. That such dealings are conducted in civil fashion and not with violence is at least partially a result of the productivity to be gained from peaceful reliance on specialization.

If we were to suppose that people favor strangers over themselves, then this too would be seen most clearly in organized markets where strangers deal with each other. It is not the market that governs what is wanted. The predilection to explain the operation of markets by assuming that people emphasize their own well-being is not a result of markets. It is a result of the fact that this supposition predicts behavior in market dealings much better than would the contrary supposition.

2 PROTECTING YOU FROM YOURSELF

I

People do sometimes misjudge what they want. They make mistakes. Yes, but this is not necessarily a mistake. Perfection in decision making is infinitely costly and consuming of time, so we are wise to accept a positive probability of error and even wiser to tolerate higher probabilities if the cost of reducing error is greater. There is nothing irrational about this, and one can interpret such mistakes as truly serving our interests, since occasionally we learn from our mistakes. This may be the most effective way to lower the cost of avoiding mistakes in the future. These considerations are neglected by most writers who think people make the wrong choices. I assume that our goal – mine, yours, and also that of those who have doubts about our choices – is efficiency, not perfection.

Now, I would not have written this essay if those who think we err more often than we should were simply stating their beliefs. Who has not given advice to others? Indeed, this essay is intended to advise its readers. And who can claim never to have made a decision that, after it was made, seems to have been unwise? I ask only that there be open competition in the advice-giving game, and, generally speaking, there is. My objection is to those who believe that we are so locked into serious decision errors that we must be coerced into doing that which we knowingly choose not to do.

I do not deny that coercion has its uses. No society tolerates complete freedom of choice; nor does one bar all free choice. The realistic issue is the mixture of free and restricted choice. The value you put on free choice will affect your notion of the proper mix, whether or not your valuation is itself correct by some standard other than your own judgment. Most societies deny free choice to children, the mentally handicapped, and those who would violate the rights of others; the adverse affects on society of murder, theft, speeding, and so on are obvious to enough people that we combine to make them illegal. So let us set aside choice restrictions of this sort and turn to the day-to-day behavior of law-abiding, normal adults; this is the group whose behavior has been targeted for alteration by coercive means by these critics of free choice.

I focus this essay on one such critic, Robert H. Frank, whose popular and successful book *Luxury Fever* (1999) calls for progressive consumption taxation as a tool by which to discourage wealthy people from purchasing luxury goods. In disagreeing with Frank, I do not thereby reject a progressive consumption tax. There are reasons for and against such a tax that are quite different from that which is used by Frank. I write few words about John K. Galbraith's *The Affluent Society* (1958) and *The New Industrial State* (1967); these also call for taxation to discourage purchases. Frank's book is center stage because it is contemporary, well written, and, in one way or another, embeds the ideas of most of his predecessors, including Veblen, whose influential *The Theory of the Leisure Class* had, in 1899, already set in place the basic arguments that later critics use. Frank's book, in addition, offers some novel considerations.

All of these writers, with their own variations, adopt Veblen's theme that our purchases fail to serve our true needs. Veblen sees this especially in the behavior of the wealthy and leisure classes, who, he claims, acquire goods and adopt manners for the purpose of signaling to others that they stand on lower rungs of the social status ladder. Unlike most of those whose writings use similar themes, Veblen is more interested in the psychology and sociology of human behavior, and in critiquing the economic model of rational behavior, than he is in policies for altering behavior. Galbraith offers two variations on Veblen's theme. People, in his *The Affluent Society*, overestimate the insecurity they face; as a result, they work harder, acquire more wealth, and husband more of this wealth than serves their own true interests.[1] In *The New Industrial State*, Galbraith modifies this theme by claiming not that people are too husbanding of their wealth but that they are led by professional advertisers, acting as agents of the technocrats who produce goods, to purchase excessive amounts of privately produced goods. He calls for taxation, the proceeds of which are to be used to supply people with publicly produced goods. Frank's theme is a blend of Veblen's and Galbraith's. The wealthy, he claims, spend more on luxury goods than the value they derive directly from these goods, doing so in an attempt to maintain, or to increase, their status in their peer group. To rectify this, Frank calls for a progressive consumption tax that will raise the cost to the wealthy of acquiring expensive luxury goods.

Frank's presence in the group of intellectuals who are of this mind is somewhat puzzling. Before he wrote *Luxury Fever*, he penned *Passions Without Reason* (1988), a fine work that offered a novel explanation for the role of emotions in human behavior. He argues that seemingly irrational emotional behavior serves us well by imprinting the minds of those with whom we have conflicts that we are committed to stand by and defend our interest. It is because this behavior cannot be justified on the basis of short-term benefits and costs of taking it (it is short-run irrational) that others take seriously the message of commitment that is delivered by way of

---

[1] My colleague Peter C. Whybrow (2005) urges a similar theme on his readers, but, unlike Galbraith and Frank, he does not call for coercive policies to rectify this behavior.

overreacting to a conflict situation. Given this insight, I would have thought Frank would be careful before labeling seemingly senseless behavior irrational, but this what he does in *Luxury Fever*.

II

Galbraith claimed in *The Affluent Society* that people had become locked into the irresistible habit of attempting to accumulate wealth. This habit, he writes, arose during the thousands of years of primitive times during which circumstances held people close to subsistence levels of nutrition. In *The New Industrial State*, he makes the acquisition of private goods, not of wealth more generally, the mistaken objective of human behavior. Somehow, primitive times plus present advertising have honed humans to prefer private over publicly produced goods, and he views this as keeping the level of publicly produced goods below optimum levels. Galbraith's solution is to raise taxes, thus reducing expenditures on privately produced goods, and to use the resources thus released to produce more publicly produced goods.

Frank modifies both presumptions, but holds to their substance, and so, too, his taxation solution. He claims that people's actions are motivated by a primitively acquired and irresistible instinct to attain higher stature than other members of their peer group. The wealthy, he claims, seek stature by acquiring more luxury goods than their rival peers. As you can see, there really isn't much difference between these views. Habit and instinct are quite substitutable and so are wealth, private goods, and luxury goods.

Competition between the wealthy causes luxury goods to be produced in quantities that Frank judges as excessive; this too is not much different from Galbraith's judgment that private goods are produced in excessive quantities, but Frank appeals to anthropological and biological studies of rivalry to win "alpha-male" positions in their peer groups to make his case, and not simply to Galbraith's assertion that humans have an inherited propensity to stay high above the poverty line.

Indeed, all three writers place a large part of the blame for our misguided behavior on natural selection; their claim is that our instinctual wants for wealth and rank, acquired during very long periods when poverty and control by force prevailed and were of service to our survival, are now ill-suited to our social arrangements and high living standards.[2] These writers do not note, and may not have recognized, that they severely reduce the role that can be played by persuasion in our affairs. We are more or less locked into ill-suited wants for the foreseeable future. Absent this condition, those who would rebut the claims of these writers would deny the necessity for using coercion. Why not rely on competitive persuasion to change people's behavior? The power of natural selection is why not.

Frank goes on to claim, as had Veblen in his *The Theory of the Leisure Class* a century earlier, that competition by the wealthy to outdo their peers in the acquisition of luxury goods is self-defeating and, hence, does not serve the personal desire for higher status. Advance in stature is achieved by doing better than other members of one's peer group, but this is difficult, even impossible, to do because all members of the group are quite capable of using considerable wealth in a competitive struggle for stature through the purchase of luxury goods. Luxury goods competition serves no useful purpose for those whose instincts drive them to compete for status, yet the production of luxury goods uses scarce resources.

The solution he proposes is a progressive consumption tax which, he claims, will reduce expenditures made by the wealthy on luxury goods. This presumption seems inconsistent with conditions that he uses to keep luxury goods competition unproductive for the wealthy. The wealthy purchase fewer luxury goods if the tax is

---

[2] Galbraith also blames persuasive advertising.

imposed. In this, they act *sensibly in response to the increased cost* to them of acquiring another unit of expensive luxury goods. However, the rationale Frank uses in calling for this tax is the inability of the wealthy to act sensibly when some within their peer group purchase luxury goods. The purchase of luxury goods by others raises the cost of advancing a "unit" in status to those who have not yet purchased luxury goods. But, rather than acting sensibly to this increase in the price of status (as Frank expects them to if they are faced with a progressive consumption tax), they respond by attempting to maintain or increase their status. The sensible response assumed in the case of the tax, if applied to luxury goods, would call for reducing the quantity or quality of luxury goods purchased. Surely, an "economizing" instinct also has been indelibly imprinted in our psyches by natural selection. Yet, in this case, unlike the taxation case, Frank neglects to recognize the economizing instinct. Selective selection substitutes for natural selection. The wealthy continue with the same intensity to indulge their desire for stature. If the wealthy cannot discipline themselves to reduce expenditures on luxury goods, why do they react sensibly to a tax-imposed increase in the cost of a unit of stature?

I have no reason to deny a role for status seeking in human behavior, although none of our authors gives evidence bearing on the importance and quantitative significance of status seeking (or, in Galbraith's case, of overpurchasing privately produced goods) or on whether seeking status really is negatively productive. The cases they make involve their beliefs, not evidence.

III

The point on which Frank's argument differs from those of his predecessors is to identify a person's expenditures on luxury goods as the source of an external cost. One wealthy person's purchase of a unit of luxury goods makes it imperative for others to make purchases that they really would prefer not to make, and Frank views this as the imposition of an external cost on them. This identification derives from his claim that the expenditure *compels* other status-seeking persons to acquire more luxury goods themselves and, thus, causes them to bear a cost they would not have borne had the initial expenditure not been made. This justifies his call for social action; without it, a participant in this contest simply bears the cost of foolishness.

It is surprising to me that Frank too broadly identifies an externality, treating it as cost that X bears as a result of an action taken by Y. Early in his book, on page 9, he writes "Adam Smith's celebrated invisible hand – the claim that society as a whole does best when individuals pursue their own interests in the open marketplace – rests on the assumption that each person's choices have no negative consequence for others." I need not rise to Smith's defense here, but he clearly recognizes that resources used in one activity have negative consequences for those who would prefer to have these resources in another activity.

More important, negative consequences for others do not necessarily result in externalities as this term is used in economics. Shifting land from wheat to corn production, say in order to produce biofuel, will raise the price of wheat, and this will make lovers of wheat products worse off. So what? Each owner of land committed to corn production faces the implicit cost of foregoing revenues he would receive from producing more wheat should he shift some of his land back to wheat production. He therefore takes the price of wheat, which measures how much wheat users are willing to pay for another bushel of wheat, into full account when he chooses to grow corn. There is a negative effect on wheat consumers, but there is no externality, and the value of the wheat that can be grown on this land is fully taken into account. Smith's awareness of the fact that scarce resources used in one activity are not available for use in another is quite clear throughout his *The Wealth of Nations*.

Frank follows this with a set of examples, some of which really are externalities, but some of which are not. "The presence of a preschooler with the chicken pox has negative consequences for others" does describe a negative consequence that is an externality. "When I stay an extra hour at the office each day . . . I reduce the promotion prospects of others, and thereby create an incentive for them to work longer hours than they otherwise would have chosen" is a negative consequence that, like the land example, is not an externality, since the cost of working harder is the amount that the worker who will not be promoted would offer to reduce the salary he asks of his employer if the promotion were his. The owner of the firm, like the owner of land, forgoes this offer, and therefore will take it into account if he chooses to promote the worker who works the extra hour.

This carelessness is not a trivial matter. The case Frank makes against the purchase of luxury goods rests on it. After all, the people that are at the center of discussion through much of his book – the wealthy – can avoid the negative consequence threatened by someone who spends a bit more on luxury goods. They simply can refuse to participate in luxury goods competition. The traditional basis for identifying a negative consequence as an external cost is that it results from an action taken by someone else that is prohibitively costly to deter, and I, but obviously not Frank, would think refusing to play the game is a simple matter.[3]

Although Frank has no explicit discussion of the cost condition required to transform a negative consequence into an externality, he implicitly conjures such a condition when he asserts that inherited instinct makes it impossible for a wealthy person (or others, I suppose) to refuse to play the game. Well, this is an externality only by assertion; we have no evidence of an inherited compulsion to compete for status by way of luxury goods acquisition, or if present, of how strong this compulsion might be.

---

[3] But see the essay on externalities, in which I argue that this cost condition overstates the importance of externalities.

It would seem much more difficult to resist paying a progressive consumption tax, but Frank does not discuss the much more plausible case for an externality in the very solution to the luxury fever problem that he proposes. After all, those who are not wealthy or, even if wealthy, who choose not to engage in luxury goods competition also bear this tax.

Frank's view would allow an expenditure made in response to *any* activity undertaken by another person to be identified as an external cost. Thus, if John has an inherited tendency to socialize with others by way of discussing books, Frank, in writing and publishing *Luxury Fever*, is imposing an external cost on John! We are left with no practical degree of free will or voluntary behavior in Frank's claims, since Frank offers no means for distinguishing some instinct-driven purchases (or actions) from others or for distinguishing instinct-driven purchases from purchases that reflect voluntary choice. "Instinct" is a powerful tool, indeed.[4]

Frank's argument is quite different from one like that which bases coercive action on the collective good nature of national defense, which claims that defense, if left to market forces, will be undersupplied. His claim is much simpler, but more difficult to accept: the wealthy, although they would benefit from withdrawing from luxury goods competition, are prevented from doing so by instinct.

He could have made a stronger argument by claiming that each wealthy person is reluctant to withdraw from luxury goods

---

[4] There appeared at the time of the writing of this essay a news story about a study undertaken at Harvard Medical School and published by the *New England Journal of Medicine*. The study claimed that fat people do harm to their close friends by making it easier for them to overeat than would be true if they dined only with thin people. Fat people, therefore, impose external costs on those with whom they dine. It may well be that people who like food very much just enjoy each other's company, but I do not judge the scientific substance, if any, in this study. It would seem to me that the cost of avoiding this association is not so great that one ought to label the consequences of being fat as an external cost imposed on others with whom a person associates. And, if avoiding a fat person is difficult because there is *greater pleasure* in dining with a person who enjoys and consumes food, then why not label this an external benefit instead of an external cost?

competition because remaining in the fray permits him to gain stature if others withdraw first. However, this supposes that the wealthy are already locked in luxury goods competition. More important, such withdrawal is contrary to his argument that the behavior that lies behind this competition is instinct driven.

IV

What is special about luxury-goods status competition, anyway? It involves nothing more than the investment of wealth in a competitive effort to win a contest that is not unlike other contests. How does it differ from the competition between baseball teams, from contests between would-be politicians for political office, or from contests between firms for market share, or from contests between students for grades? Most impertinent of all, how does it differ from competition between economists for the Nobel Prize? I see no obvious differences, since participation in all these contests can be rationalized as stature-seeking rivalry. Trot out an instinct-driven desire to compete for status, extending the reach of Frank's argument, and all these forms of competition become unproductive uses of resources in Frank's calculus unless they offer merits he does not find in luxury goods competition.

Such merits would be of two types. It might be possible actually to gain status. Luxury goods competition is unproductive in this dimension because Frank supposes that no one can win. Factually, this may be incorrect. One baseball team does win the World Series, and one team, the New York Yankees, has won a disproportionate number of times. Why, then, is it impossible for one wealthy person to win the game? Remember, winning is a matter of relative achievement. It means only that more luxury goods have been acquired than have been acquired by the nearest rival; it does not require a substantial margin between the winner and the follower-up. If some students do better than others on exams, what is it that bars some wealthy persons from doing better than others in the luxury-goods status game?

Frank gives no real explanation for the absence of a winner except to appeal, inappropriately, to a model of interaction much like the perfect competition model; all he tells us is that all wealthy people can match the expenditures of others. Well, I am not so sure this is true, any more than I am that all economists can just as easily put time, effort, and intelligence into a career designed to win approval from the Nobel Prize committee. Not all wealthy persons have the same wealth, taste, and intensity of interest in status. Why should all do equally well in this game? And if some can do better than others, well, then, the game does have a productivity element in it for those who play it. Moreover, competing in this game, quite aside from winning it, may make life more interesting and exciting for those who play it, an aspect of productivity neglected by Frank.

The second potential source of productivity is found in how the game affects those who do not play it. What, after all, is a luxury good? Printed books once were only for the wealthy, but now books are within the reach of virtually everyone in Western societies; so it is with radios, television sets, refrigerators, automobiles, and medical procedures. The most prized luxury good at the turn of the century, found only in the homes of the very wealthy, was indoor plumbing. Many goods begin commercial life as luxuries priced beyond the reach of commoners. Motorola's first commercial cell phone, introduced in 1984, was priced at $3,995. However, purchases by the few who are wealthy soon become purchases by the many not so wealthy. The few demonstrate to the many and also to potential and actual producers that these goods are (or that they are not) reliably functional; these few serve as risk takers for the many. The conviction that novel goods are functional makes it reasonable to increase production and thereby reduce unit cost. The purchase of luxury goods by the wealthy begins a process of making new goods available at reduced prices to others. These goods soon become "run-of-the-mill." The not-so-wealthy would need to wait longer and pay more for less if the wealthy did not purchase novel goods, a consequence that would follow were Frank to be successful in securing a progressive tax on consumption.

Moreover, aside from easing novel goods into the inventories of the not-so-wealthy, we benefit from efforts made by people to become wealthy even if they are motivated to make these efforts in order to out-status others. One source of benefits is found in the most-used route to wealth: productive entrepreneurial activity. McCormack may have developed the reaper simply to win wealth-associated status, but his work had profound effects on reducing the extent of poverty in the world. Those who seek to become wealthy do so mostly by bearing entrepreneurial risks that ordinary folks shun, and the net result of their risk bearing has been to make the rest of us better off.

A second source of benefits is found in expenditures of the wealthy that Frank neglects. Carnegie brought a giant steel firm into existence and became wealthy in doing so, but he used a part of his wealth to create a system of open-access libraries through-out the land. Rockefeller created the University of Chicago. Even if wealth is used to purchase luxury goods, it is also used in these socially useful ways. And I would think that the way to status most favored by the wealthy is not the acquisition of more luxury goods but by outdoing rivals in the giving of wealth to others who can put it to uses that serve society at large.

A third way the rest of us might benefit from efforts to gain status through the acquisition of wealth, and perhaps the most important benefit, is that it channels the competition for status into directions that, compared with others, are benign. Frank and others see human behavior, or at least a part of it and at least for some, as determined by a biologically determined urge to acquire status. There are many ways to attempt to satisfy this urge, and some of these are much more dangerous than playing the luxury goods game. The alpha male seeks power, not luxury goods. So did

Stalin, Hitler, and Capone. Luxury fever offers a fairly innocent path for status seeking. Policies that ban it, such as those used by Mao in seeking cultural revolution in China, redirect status-seeking efforts toward acquiring power over others. Even if Frank's attack on luxury fever were correct in its claims, competition among the wealthy to acquire luxury goods serves society by channeling status rivalry away from competition to acquire power over others.

By now, readers know full well that I do not think much of Frank's attack on the behavior of the wealthy, but I mostly object to his call for a tax policy that aims to change this behavior. Readers are entitled to disagree, but I ask them to consider seriously if his claims are sufficiently strong and meritorious to warrant restrictions on free choice. The behavior we are discussing is not the equivalent of cigarette smoking, with its associated ill-effects on the health of those who smoke and, assertedly, on others who do not. He is discussing the tendency of the wealthy to purchase more expensive goods than are purchased by the not so wealthy. Even if his argument were well founded in fact and in reasoning, it offers a weak case for limiting choice in a society that values freedom highly. Purchase of expensive goods by wealthy people may not be wise, but it does not injure them or others. No one becomes a burden of the state as a result of such behavior. Free choice is much too precious to surrender just because the wealthy buy more expensive goods than some of us think they should. Frank is entitled to his disdain of such behavior and to preach to the wealthy, but the free society does not entitle him to coerce them into submission to his idea of what is good for them.

3 RESCUING ECONOMIC MAN FROM
THE SELFISH GENE

T HE FOCUS ON ECONOMIC MAN IN ESSAY 1 MAY HAVE BEEN OUT of place. The biologist Richard Dawkins (1976) claims that the *person* is but the agent of his or her genes. Gene interests guide human action. And, unlike the critics discussed in the prior essay, who claim that people do not choose goals that truly serve their interests, the theory of the selfish gene leaves no doubt about the gene serving its purpose; natural selection has made survival this purpose. Selfish-gene theory may topple the person, but it strengthens the case for the power of self-interest as this is measured by gene interest.

My objectives here are two. First, I examine some implications of selfish-gene theory that are not explicit in Dawkins's work, or in those parts of the debate that has followed publication of his work that I have been able to read. Second, I extricate economic man from the agent status to which he is assigned by selfish-gene theory. The gene of Dawkins's theory is entirely focused on one goal – its survival. Survival certainly is important to economic man, but, as viewed in economics, it is not his exclusive goal. Superficially viewed, people seem willing to take risks they would avoid if survival were their only goal. People are willing to court the risk of dying to experience the exhilaration of climbing high mountains; to get from here to there faster than is safe; and to undertake dangerous voyages across unknown seas and even through unexplored space. People charge into a hail of bullets coming from enemy machine guns; and, on occasion, they take their own lives. In contrast, they press hard to live well beyond their child-bearing years and even beyond the years in which they can do any good for themselves or others. Economists view these activities, and a variety of those that are more mundane, as reflecting the multi-faceted nature of human wants, but they offer no explanation of why these wants are part of human psychology. Wants, in all their diversity, are taken as given, as revealed by behavior itself. Biologists, in contrast, see the underlying source of wants in natural selection. This is why they hold tenaciously to the goal of explaining all behavior in terms of survival (of the person, the gene, or the species). Behavior incompatible with survival is not long tolerated by natural selection.

It is not difficult to understand the reason for this difference in viewpoint. The two disciplines have different basic problems. Economics seeks, or has sought, to understand resource allocation by way of markets and prices, and to a large extent this problem can be viewed in static terms. Take technology and *wants* as given (and as revealed) and then deduce the resource allocation that results from the use of prices and markets in a decentralized economy. The imagination of biologists has been captured by the problem of speciation, a problem whose central features are change through time in characteristics of organisms.

However, in discussions of their central problems, both disciplines have had difficulties with behavior that appears altruistic. Truly altruistic behavior seems inconsistent with both economic man's maximization of his own welfare and biological man's maximization of survival probability. The *truly* altruistic act, by definition, reduces the aid giver's welfare (or probability of surviving) in order to increase that of the aid receiver. A main objective of Dawkins's work is to demonstrate that behavior that is self-sacrificing from the perspective of the person giving aid, and which in fact is detrimental to this person's survival, can be self-serving and survival-enhancing from the perspective of his genes. If this view is correct, altruistic behavior no longer is puzzling for biologists.

This essay is much more likely to be read by people who are not biologists and by people who, although they have read Dawkins's work, no longer recall its details clearly, so there is reason to begin with a brief summary of his theory as I understand it.

I

Dawkins views the gene as the unit of life relevant to the transmission of organism characteristics from the present generation to the future generation and, hence, to Dawkins, the gene is the unit of life relevant to natural selection. If there is an increase in the probability that the information encoded in a gene survives, the action that brings about this increase serves the selfish interest of the gene. He replaces the survival-seeking person (or other organism) with the survival-seeking gene, claiming that the person is agent of the gene. He then demonstrates that gene survival can be promoted by actions that jeopardize the survival of the person giving the aid.

Altruism can be gene serving because some of the genes in the aid giver may have identical matches in the aid receiver. Identical matches encode the same information. All the genes of one identical twin, for example, are the same as those of the other twin. In this special case, an altruistic-seeming action taken by one twin toward the other is selfish if this action is expected to increase the probability that the aided twin survives by more than it increases the probability that the aiding twin does not survive, since, on this probability trade-off, there is an increase in the probability that information encoded in the genes of both twins survives.

Identical twins are a special case in that there is no doubt about their genes being identical. In the more general case, the probability that identical genes are embodied in aid giver and aid receiver will be greater the more closely they are related biologically. The conditions under which an altruistic-seeming act is interpretable as selfish involve (1) the effect of this act on the survival probabilities of the interacting people and (2) the likelihood that these people embody identical genes. An aid giver puts herself and her genes in jeopardy when undertaking dangerous (or costly) actions that increase the survival probability of an aid receiver. The increase in survival probability of the aid receiver may exceed the increase in the probability that the aid giver does not survive; this is a necessary but not a sufficient condition for the altruistic act to be interpreted as selfish. Yet to be determined is the probability that the two people embody identical genes; this probability is greater the more closely the interacting people are biologically related to each other.

An altruistic-seeming action taken under conditions that are suitable in these two respects can be interpreted as selfish because Dawkins makes the mover of the action the gene, not the person. It is somewhat more accurate to make the information encoded in a gene the mover of the action, since the survival of this information is what affects the substance of life in the future. The survival of this information is assured by survival of the identical gene "copy" embodied in either the aid giver or aid receiver, and altruistic action promotes this survival if the copy in the receiver of aid experiences an increase in survival probability greater, in absolute terms, than the decrease in survival probability of the copy in the aid giver.[1]

---

[1] Dawkins is not the first scholar who argues that there are selfish reasons for seemingly altruistic behavior. Adam Smith, who published *The Wealth of Nations* in 1776, exactly two centuries before Dawkins's *The Selfish Gene* appeared, performs a similar alchemy by portraying altruism as motivated by the self-interested seeking of stature and of respect from others; he even offers an explanation for why this pathway to stature is more effective the more closely related are aid giver and aid receiver. And, by the way, he uses these same goals, stature and respect, to explain why people are willing to work so hard and to bear such large risks in order to acquire great wealth when *great* wealth, as compared to more modest wealth, improves living circumstances only slightly.

II

Dawkins's theory is focused on a subset of genes that I label *family-ancestral*. These differentiate one family from another and one family history from another. Dawkins does not give much justification for this focus, pausing only to say the following:

> For simplicity I shall assume that we are talking about genes that are rare in the gene pool as a whole.... Now the important point is that even a gene that is rare in the population as a whole is common within a family.
>
> (Dawkins, 1989, p. 90)

If this brief rationale is neither clear nor convincing, it does serve to yield deductions that are consistent with an important fact about altruistic behavior: altruism occurs more frequently between people who are closely related biologically than between those who are not. The probability that a family-ancestral gene residing in the prospective aid giver has an identical match in the prospective receiver is greater the more closely related biologically are the people. The probability is 1 if the interacting people are identical twins, 0.50 if they are ordinary siblings, 0.25 if they are first cousins, and so on.[2]

However, the probability that family-ancestral genes exist in two related people can be greater than these numbers indicate, since the parents of two siblings, for example, may themselves share a common family ancestry. This would be true for parents who are cousins, for example. This raises an issue that will be discussed later, since biologists now seem to believe that all humans are descended from a common parent or a few sets of parents. For present

---

[2] This difference in frequency, of course, might be attributed to the statistical fact that close relations are more often in the position of seeking and giving aid to each other, but a more careful consideration of this fact suggests that something more than statistics is at work. I will argue later that this "more" is a theory that differs from selfish-gene theory.

purposes, however, I abide by Dawkins's desire to focus on genes that are family-ancestral in a way that meets his notion.

These family-ancestral genes fall into two categories, those that are identical in the interacting people and those that are not. Ordinary siblings will embody some of both these categories. Stylistic shortcuts are useful here because I intend to make more of the difference between these two categories of genes than does Dawkins. In accord with this, as between aid giver and aid receiver, let *HIC* and *NHIC*, respectively, symbolize held in common family-ancestral genes and not held in common genes. HIC genes, in Dawkins's terminology, are identical genes embodied in different people. The physical copies of the HIC genes that reside in an aid giver and an aid receiver are in fact different; one copy may die while the other lives. Yet, both encode information that calls for production of the same protein. If the conditions of selfish-gene theory are met, an altruistic action will increase the probability that this protein remains embedded in future generations. A sufficient condition for this to be the case when the two people are identical twins is that the altruistic action promotes survival of the aid-receiving twin more than it compromises survival of the aid-giving twin. This is insufficient, though still necessary, when the relationship between people is more distant than it is for identical twins, since the greater the biological difference between the interacting people, the smaller the probability that they embody identical genes. For this reason, Dawkins's focus on family-ancestral genes implies a correlation between frequency of altruistic behavior and closeness of biological relationship.[3]

Little attention is given by Dawkins to those genes that are NHIC, although he makes reference to work of others relating

---

[3] This is the rationale behind the so-called R criterion for – seemingly – altruistic action to take place: R is 1.0 for identical twins, 2.0 for ordinary siblings, 4.0 for first cousins and so on.

to competition between genes. The interests of NHIC genes seem worthy of more attention, since only identical twins hold all genes in common. Consider people who, though they may be related, are not identical twins. At least some genes embodied in these people are NHIC. NHIC genes embodied in the aid giver are put into jeopardy if he or she undertakes an altruistic action, and so the information they encode is less likely to survive. These genes seem to be "unwilling altruists" drawn into a dangerous position by HIC genes. (The NHIC genes embodied in the aided person, of course, have no objection to receiving aid, since their survival probability will increase.)

Even though the aid giver's NHIC genes are jeopardized by an altruistic act, they may have "approved" it before the act is taken. No gene knows if it will be HIC or NHIC until the act is performed. Prior to the act, all genes in the prospective aid giver will approve the taking of the action if they "believe" that the probability of HIC being present in the aid receiver is high enough to compensate for the risk they face of discovering ex post that they are NHIC. Dawkins does not explain how this assessment is made, a topic I return to below, but each gene in the giver will assent to the altruistic action if it promises an *expected* increase in survival probability. We may note here that this decision-making procedure (unlike the private-ownership economic model to be discussed later in these essays) demands uniformity of "opinion" across all genes in the aid giver, whether or not this opinion is "give aid" or "do not give aid." In the absence of uniformity of opinion, there must be some (unspecified by Dawkins) way to weight the opposing opinions of different genes.[4] On the basis of the uniformity of opinion criterion, the action is reasonably interpreted as reflecting a selfish interest in preserving information encoded on each of the

---

[4] Presumably, natural selection will lead to the adoption of a weighting system that is evolutionarily stable.

aid giver's genes. The action once taken delivers this expectation for HIC genes only, so NHIC genes embodied in the aid giver are in fact jeopardized by the action.

That NHIC genes residing in the aid giver are put into jeopardy has empirical consequences that go unrecognized in Dawkins's exposition. These arise if the positions of aid giver and aid receiver reflect a systematic selection process. Unhealthy people, for example, are more likely to find themselves in need of aid; healthy people are more likely to find themselves capable of extending aid. The gene that differentiates between good and poor health often will be NHIC, in which case the altruistic action will reduce the probability that good health is passed to future generations; eugenics by way of altruism instead of by way of sexual reproduction. Of course, the health-differentiating gene could be HIC, and in this case the altruistic interaction will promote the health of future generations by increasing the probability that information encoded in this gene survives. However, good-health genes are more likely to be NHIC, since the person in need of aid is more likely to be of poorer health than the person extending the aid. Wealth status should produce a similar outcome if (1) wealthy people are more likely to be givers than takers of aid and (2) genetic characteristics associated with the ability to acquire wealth are more likely to be found in NHIC than in HIC genes. Altruistic action in this case, since it reduces the survival of NHIC genes in the aid giver but promotes the survival of all genes in the aid receiver, will tend to make future generations poorer than they would be if altruism did not occur. The effect on future generations in this respect, of course, is different if genes that make wealth acquisition more likely are HIC, but, as with health-associated genes, this is not likely to be the case. This suggests that a somewhat different process, one that attenuates these deleterious effects, will be favored by natural selection. These inferences cannot be derived from an approach to gene survival that is focused narrowly on the interests of only the HIC genes.[5]

III

The discussion to this point, as in Dawkins's work, has focused on family-ancestral genes, but the logic of selfish-gene theory imposes no such focus. It applies equally well to genes that are not family-ancestral. No reason provided by the theory dictates that the demand for survival should be relevant only for genes that are related through family (as family is meant by Dawkins). All that matter is identicalness, and genes can be identical even if they are not embedded in relatives. The offspring of a given pair of parents hold, in a probabilistic sense, *at least* 50 percent of their genes in common, but they may hold more than 50 percent in common. This will be the case if the parents are themselves linked ancestrally. This is recognized by Dawkins. The question left unexamined by Dawkins is how to define the family.

On the assumption that there is only a single organism or only a very few organisms from which we are all descended, it would seem that ancestral linkage might be more significant than Dawkins's exposition of selfish-gene theory suggests. We belong to the same species, and "species" is meaningless if it does not mean (a broadly conceived notion of) family. True differences in ancestry can arise only if inherited genes are modified through mutation and errors in copying and location, for these alterations will make one person and one family line different from another. Let us suppose that

---

5 The particular examples chosen to illustrate this point, health and wealth, also suggest another implication. It is not unreasonable to suppose that health and wealth are causatively associated with the probability that a person survives. Survival of their genes is jeopardized in these two cases, but this process, should it continue through several generations, ends up by reducing survival probability even for the HIC genes of the future. HIC genes are "calling the tune" in regard to the taking of altruistic action. If the conditions just laid out were really do exist, the interests of HIC genes eventually would be undermined by natural selection.

such alterations are absent. The offspring of one pair of parents will then hold all or many (if we derive from more than one set of origin parents) genes in common with offspring of other parents. In this case, selfish-gene theory would not imply differences in frequency of altruistic behavior between people related through the same parents as between people related through different parents. The correlation between frequency of altruistic interaction and (conventional) biological relationship called for by Dawkins's narrower concept of family would not exist. If it does exist, the rate of drop-off in frequency of altruistic interaction as (conventional) relationship becomes more distant would depend on the general fraction of human genes that have gone through the alteration process noted above. In general, this would be a smaller rate of drop-off than is suggested by the narrower notion of family used by Dawkins.

It is useful now to repeat the citation given earlier from Dawkins's book when he explains his focus on family-differentiating genes:

For simplicity I shall assume that we are talking about genes that are rare in the gene pool as a whole.... Now the important point is that even a gene that is rare in the population as a whole is common within a family.

The genes he refers to as rare in the gene pool would seem to be those that, through generations, have been altered in ways suggested above. Genes that have not been so altered remain HIC across individuals even if these individuals are of different immediate parentage, and these genes, in addition to family-ancestral genes, will seek survival. True, the altered genes defined as family-ancestral are more likely to find identical genes in close family members, since relatives are more likely to carry the same altered genes, but even genes that have not been altered will find identical genes in people who are not (as well as people who are) close family members. The probability that one gene finds an identical gene in another person is greater the more closely the two people are related, but, and this is key, this probability would not seem to increase as much as is supposed by Dawkins's exposition of selfish-gene theory. The theory Dawkins sets, in contrast to his description of this theory, implies that the frequency of selfish altruism will not increase as rapidly with closeness of biological relationship in the sense this is meant by Dawkins.[6]

I know of no reason to doubt that the increase in frequency of altruism with biological closeness is in fact less than that which is called for by the way Dawkins calculates biological distance. However, as I have just claimed, the increase should be less sharp because many human genes have not gone through an altering process. If I am correct, the empirically documented increase in frequency is to be explained by a theory different from selfish-gene theory. What might this be?

IV

Dawkins does not give a solid explanation of the way in which genes recognize the presence of identical matches in other people. He does not specify a mechanism for enabling a direct process of recognition and assessment and, since none seems apparent, let us assume that none exists. Genes then need an indirect process for accomplishing these tasks. They need an agent, one that senses and thinks well enough to evaluate and properly to act on opportunities to interact altruistically. In the case of human genes, this agent is the "person" in which they reside. Agents, however, are not free. Not only must they be maintained, but they also bring agency-type problems with them. They may behave in ways that suit them, and what suits them may not always be what would suit the genes who

---

[6] That genes in identical twins are all HIC is due to the absence of enough time to allow for a significant probability that exogenous forces cause the genes of identical twins to begin to differ.

reside as principals within them. The existence of a degree of discord between agent and principals is explained by the necessity for giving the person a degree of freedom in ferreting out opportunities and acting on them. Without such freedom, the agent would need to be programmed in great detail, and the programmers – the person's genes – would need to anticipate all that the person may encounter. This would be more costly to the genes than bearing a measure of discord between their immediate interests and those of a person who is endowed with a measure of freedom. If the person is to generally act in the interest of embodied genes, the person must be made responsive to worldly incentives that will produce rough agreement between the person's interests and actions and the interests of his or her genes.

The set of incentives that serves this need will be a product of natural selection, since incorrect incentives will generally work against the survival of embodied genes. People who act in complete disregard of the survival of embodied genes put these genes in jeopardy, but so do people who refuse to exercise a degree of freedom and who, instead, require direct, detailed, and costly instruction from their genes. Natural selection will favor the survival of genes embodied in people in whom there is some probability of conflict between the short-run, immediate interests of the genes and the desires and actions of the people in whom they reside.

One source of such conflict is a difference in the expected life spans of people and genes. Dawkins's claim is that genes are the unit of life most relevant to natural selection because, among other reasons, they are capable of surviving for an indefinitely long time. People, on the other hand, have much shorter expected lives. As biologists recognize, it would be wasteful to design people so as to support the possibility of an indefinite life when they in fact face positive probabilities of starving, becoming deathly ill, suffering accidents, and being consumed by predators. While it is true that the specific genes embodied in people subject to such calamities also die, the information they embody can survive in people who do not experience these calamities. Genes, therefore, have a longer expected life than people. Possessed of a body that is not only designed to wear out more quickly than its genes wear out, but also is more subject to destruction by accident and by attack, the person, acting in his or her own interest, will generally be more adverse to actions whose benefits would be realized at a future time beyond that for which the body is designed but not beyond that for which the genes are designed. Altruistic behavior in fact reduces the survival probability of an aid giver; people who contemplate giving aid to others will not in fact give aid unless the trade-off between the reduced probability of their survival and the increased probability of survival of the recipients of aid is more advantageous to the aid givers than is the trade-off that their genes would find acceptable.

Natural selection will favor people who, for one reason or another, are able to reduce the severity of this discord, since it is gene survival that will determine which characteristics of people are carried into the future. Some form of compensating people for taking greater risks would seem needed. And here we introduce a method of compensation that modifies, perhaps even substitutes for, selfish-gene theory. Compensation from people to be aided, paid to people who provide the aid, offers such encouragement. The compensation may take many forms, including future payments, but it cannot be greater than the value assigned to the aid by those aided. The times at which the aid is received by aid givers cannot exceed their relevant realization period. (This is an issue too complicated to tackle here without specifying what people want; if people put value on the conditions in which their decedents find themselves, the realization period can extend beyond the aid giver's survival.) People will insist on a measure of reciprocity from those they aid. The receipt of this aid may prolong the aid giver's expected life or it may satisfy other dimensions of his or her well-being.

The use of a reciprocity method for allocating aid will reduce the overall frequency of seemingly altruistic action-taking as compared to the frequency that genes would prefer if they could *without cost* gain knowledge and take actions that selfish-gene theory requires. The *efficient* frequency, however, must take such costs into account. Economics, and biology also, demands efficiency, not the impossible. The frequency of seemingly altruistic action that results from the reciprocity method will be greater, and better for gene survival, than would the smaller frequency that would result if "nature" had barred compensation. In terms of *gene* survival, natural selection will favor people who value multidimensional compensation over those who value only their own survival. If well-being is served in ways other than just by way of survival, such people will, in return for compensation, be willing to accept a smaller probability of personal survival. The multiplicy of wants that is assumed in economics is not at odds with, and, indeed, is of service to, biology in resolving the agency problem that is embedded in selfish-gene theory.

V

The reciprocity theory of altruistic behavior, moreover, can explain the steep drop-off in frequency of altruism that comes with increasing biological distance between aid giver and aid receiver, where, here, biological distance is measured in accord with Dawkins's notion of family. This steep drop, the reader will remember, is inconsistent with the broader, species-relevant notion of family.

Reciprocity is not costless. Opportunities to secure adequate reciprocation must be found and the future behavior of aid receivers must be monitored if the implicitly promised reciprocal payment is to be realized. These will be smaller the closer and the more durable is the association between potential aid giver and aid receiver. A lasting, close association creates knowledge about people, about how honest they are, and about the conditions under which they now and might live. It is more difficult (costly) to secure this knowledge from a potential aid receiver who is a stranger than from one who is a close relative or long-time associate; this is to be attributed to the familiarity that durable, close association brings and not to the closeness of the biological relationship itself. Close association also makes it easier for an aid giver to establish the authenticity of the claimed need and the probability that the aid is actually put to the use claimed by the aid receiver.

These costs are worth bearing if they are expected to return a still larger benefit to the aid giver. The benefit is in the nature of an implicit obligation the aid receiver assumes when accepting aid. It may take a variety of forms, including the return of favors, a willingness of the aid receiver to extend aid in the future to the aid giver, and the attainment of status within the group to which both aid giver and aid receiver belong. Close association reduces the cost of monitoring and controlling future behavior of the aid recipient and thereby makes altruism more likely.[7]

In these ways, biological closeness (interpreted as does Dawkins) correlates with altruistic interaction, but it does so in a way that is not entirely causal. The causal relationship that would be displayed if gene survival was the only objective would be that which accords with gene identicalness, whether or not the copy genes belong to the same family-ancestral group as this has been interpreted by Dawkins; the broader and more relevant notion of the species as family does not call for so steep a drop-off in frequency of altruism as biological distance increases as that which is called for by Dawkins's narrower notion of family. Nonetheless, we do observe this steeper drop-off. It results from the informational and monitoring advantages offered by close and continuing association, and

---

[7] Reciprocity received may be viewed as improving the survival of the aid giver's genes, but, as noted already, there is no reason to deny that some benefit furthers goals other than personal survival. Nonetheless, should we wish to focus on gene survival, we see that the change in gene survival that results from the giving of aid is itself dependent on the magnitude and reliability of the expected reciprocal benefits.

this is generally associated with familial relationship. As a byproduct of these advantages, a largely incidental correlation between altruism and biological closeness arises.

The strength of this incidental correlation will be weaker if alternative sources of close, continuing association are available. These alternatives are available even if they sometimes are less reliable than is biological relationship. Soldiers serving in the same platoon for a year or more are more likely to aid members of the platoon than strangers or other military personnel. They have been trained to take care of each other *because* they themselves are likely to require aid from their fellow platoon members in the future. Clear reciprocity! The training works because platoon members remain in close association, come to know and influence each other, and find it easier to monitor future behavior of each other. Other such examples can be given. These deviations from what would be expected from selfish-gene theory, as exposited by Dawkins, are in the direction of reducing the rate of increase in frequency of altruism associated with familial relationship, and they bring the observed frequency into closer accord with what we might expect from the more broadly conceived species-related notion of family. However, these alternative sources of durable association will not generally be as prevalent and strong as those that arise from the propensity of people to stay in close association with family members. As a result, the correlation between frequency of altruistic interaction and closeness of family relationship will dominate the statistics, but will do so for reasons other than, or in addition to, those given by selfish-gene theory.

Man as seeker and user of reciprocal benefits for the bearing of risk in altruistic interactions is economic man. He appears in this story as an *efficient* agent in the service of the survival needs of his (or her) genes; consciousness and freedom of action are favored by natural selection because these make the servicing of gene survival needs efficient. As a seeker of multidimensional well-being willing to realize well-being through exchange, economic man reduces the gap that would otherwise exist between the frequency of altruism that suits him and the frequency of altruism that would in an idealized situtaiton suit his genes. The manner of accomplishing this, however, may not at all be like that depicted by selfish-gene theory. At its base, selfish-gene theory also rests on reciprocity; one gene copy receives help from another gene copy because the aid-receiving gene can do a better job of preserving information that both genes embody.

4 ECONOMIC MAN'S ESCAPE FROM MALTHUS'S POPULATION TRAP

THE PURSUIT OF ONE'S NARROWLY DEFINED SELF-INTEREST MAY sometimes come at the expense of the group to which one belongs. It is easy to give examples of this. A person in possesion of important military secrets finds it in his or her interest to offer them for sale to an enemy nation, putting his or her own country into jeopardy; at the other extreme, a person, too lazy to look for a trash can, tosses gum wrappers onto a public sidewalk. Between these two examples is the driver who enters a freeway without concern for the added congestion this causes others. These examples illustrate that Adam Smith's most important insight might not always hold under some circumstances. This insight – the invisible hand that transforms private actions into social benefits – would seem to require a set of constraints whose effects are to put private actions to the service of the larger public, and, in Smith's defense, he discovers the invisible hand in the context of the constraints imposed by the legal arrangements that underlie a market-based economy. These discourage theft and disregard for the property of others. The world being as it is, strict conditions of ownership and contract cannot be satisfied perfectly, and, so, situations do arise in which private interests may fail to serve the interests of others in the group to which one belongs.

I

The group to which I refer above is the general public, but it also can be a much smaller group that contains a few people who strive to realize the benefits of cooperation. Matt Ridley (1996), in his discussion of the intellectual history of prisoner dilemma problems, gives a prisoners' dilemma interpretation of the problem faced by a tribe setting out on a cooperative effort to acquire deer meat. Ridley attributes the example to Rousseau. As Ridley describes it:

[S]uppose everybody in the tribe goes out to hunt a stag. They do so by forming a wide ring around the thicket in which the stag is lying, and walking inwards until the beast is finally forced to try to escape from the encircling cordon of hunters, at which point, if all goes well, it is killed by the closest hunter. But suppose one of the hunters encounters a hare. He can catch the hare for sure, but only by leaving the circle. That in turn leaves a gap through which the stag escapes. The hunter who caught the hare is all right – he has meat – but everybody else pays with an empty belly the price of his selfishness. The right decision for the individual is the wrong one for the group, so proving what a hopeless product social cooperation is, said misanthropic Rousseau bleakly.

The conclusion drawn by Rousseau, and presumably by Ridley, is that the tribe abandons deer hunts because of such defections or, at least, that it suffers a reduction in the rate at which hunting efforts yield deer meat. However, this conclusion ignores larger possibilities. The correct conclusion may be a meeting of tribal leaders that sets a steep penalty for anyone caught abandoning his position in the deer hunt, perhaps a penalty that exacts two fingers from the hands of such a person. The implicit contract between tribe members that calls for serious participation of group members in the hunt becomes more effective as a result. Whereas the narrowly conceived approach to the prisoners' dilemma ends in an unfruitful search for individually played strategies of people already entrapped in the dilemma, the more productive use of the dilemma is as a guide to measures that reduce the cost of contract and ownership. And this brings us to the institutional changes that helped release mankind from Malthus's population trap. Malthus believed that the private decisions about childbearing held a society to a subsistence standard of living, a belief that many share today. The decision to bear a child is like the decision, in the deer hunt case, to go for the rabbit, the result of which is to impoverish the larger group.

II

Adam Smith and Thomas Malthus differed in their forecasts of mankind's future. Smith (1776), in his *Wealth of Nations*, offered an optimistic view, basing this on his understanding of the new economic system that began its emergence in England during his lifetime. Malthus, who wrote his famous *Essay on Population* twenty-two years after Smith's great work, offered a pessimistic view, basing this on his understanding of the past. At the time Malthus wrote, the evidence in support of his view was nothing less than what then was the entire prior history of mankind as we now know it. Smith's view, in contrast, was a product of his vision and a bare few decades of data.

Malthus believed that population not only *could* grow faster than productivity but that it *would* grow faster whenever prosperity became the condition of life. The biological propensity of people to engage sexually and to reproduce may be interpreted as the pursuit of self-interest, perhaps of the self-interest of a person's genes. (See the essay in this volume on selfish-gene theory.) The resulting growth in population, according to Malthus, works to the disadvantage of society because it undermines prosperity and brings about a poverty-caused struggle for existence. Prosperity, in Malthus's view, is a temporary affair at best. The long-term condition of mankind is poverty, not progress, unless human behavior is changed. Malthus saw little hope for this, although he did preach abstinence and delayed marriage. Everyone might resolve to abide by Malthus's sermons, just as everyone in Rousseau's deer hunt might agree not to defect in an attempt to catch a rabbit, but individuals just cannot resist when confronted with an easy rabbit or an easy sexual encounter. Yet, unlike my suggestion that society should impose a penalty on defectors, societies of that time, unlike China today, did not impose one on families that have "too many" children. As I argue next, no such specific response was necessary; the emergence of capitalism and democracy served this purpose.

Malthus's view of technical change was based on what seemed to be the slow pace at which agricultural productivity had improved through time. Additional food, on this reading of history, is secured mainly by bringing more labor and land to the task of farming. A doubling of population, assuming an equal doubling of land, holding land quality constant, brings forth only a doubling of food supply, but fails to improve living standards. A doubling of population reduces living standards if superior land is in short supply or if agricultural productivity fails to double. Darwin's writings had not yet appeared, but the Malthusian view of human behavior is much like that which would be brought forward by natural selection – the fit survive and multiply. Mankind's history prior to the nineteenth century generally supports this view. However, Malthus, thinking in terms of economics, gave attention to the living standard implied by human reproduction capability. From the nineteenth century onward, at least in the West, human behavior increasingly reflects concerns about living standard. In the years following Malthus's essay, up to contemporary times, per capita wealth has progressed upward for peoples of capitalism-favoring nations. It did so alongside trend increases in Western population. Population growth failed to undermine the rise in living standard as it should have if Malthus's beliefs were correct. One can argue that the Industrial Revolution, based on the institutions of capitalism, allowed labor productivity to grow faster than population could grow. It is true that productivity did increase, and over short periods of time, such as a decade, it sometimes increased rapidly. This might explain matters as the nineteenth century turned into the twentieth, but Malthus's predictions are rejected from the time he wrote to the time this essay is written. On a long-term-trend basis, labor productivity grows by perhaps one to two percent, rates that are surely less than the biological rate at which population can grow under conditions of prosperity. Rapid technical change, which did come with capitalism, cannot itself explain the long-term failure of Malthus's predictions.

The resolution of this puzzle may be found in another set of facts. This accompanied the growth in per capita wealth but is different from it. Family size, strangely enough, began decreasing shortly after Malthus published his essay; and it has continued to decrease to the present time. The reading of his essay may have put couples to sleep, but not quickly enough to have this effect.[1] The simultaneous increase in per capita wealth and decrease in family size seems inconsistent with Malthus's ideas and with those that many of us would hold. Good times should encourage higher birth rates and higher child survival rates; family size, one would think, should have been increasing. Family size decreased while per capita wealth and total population increased. The growth rate of population, however, began to fall and, in contemporary times, has hovered around zero in economies based on the institutions of capitalism. The key to the declining rate of increase in total population lies in the decrease in family size, and the key to the decrease in family size lies in capitalism's effect on legislation.

---

[1] Not expecting people to engage in population control, Malthus, hoping to change sexual habits, called for abstinence and late marriages, but, consistent with the theory he set forth in the first edition of his essay, he showed little confidence that people would heed his call. He was more hopeful for population control by the time the second edition of his essay was published.

New data hinting at these facts began arriving shortly after Malthus published his first essay. Critics of the essay pointed to these data to support their optimistic views of mankind's future. Malthus initially engaged them in debate but, faced with contrary data, he (reluctantly, I think) gave a happier view of mankind's future in successful rewrites of his initial essay. In these he conceded that people seemed capable of responding to social pleadings to delay marriage, have fewer children per family, and avoid out-of-wedlock births. Why socially conscious pleadings went unheeded during the long, long period prior to the time that Malthus wrote is not a question that Malthus put to himself or to his critics. A commonly expressed judgment attributed the continuing improvement in living standards to rapid technological progress as well as to improved social consciousness, but this prompts repetition of the question just asked. Why should technological progress suddenly accelerate in the nineteenth century? In any case, technological progress, although it may bring prosperity, does not lead to zero rate of growth in total population or to reductions in family size.

To explain the data in these ways, it is necessary for rapid technological improvements to be accompanied by greater willingness to respond to pleas for social consciousness when deciding on number of offspring. I do not deny a role for these conditions. The rise of capitalism surely did facilitate and reflect rapid technological improvement; pleas for socially conscious behavior certainly did not diminish as capitalism matured. Even so, standing alone, they fail to explain the timing and, in historic terms, the quickness of the breakout from Malthus's population trap as measured by per capita wealth and persistence of growth in population. After all, technology was progressing rather continuously before, during, and after the nineteenth century, but family size suddenly changed course during that century and began a long decline that was contrary to past behavior of family size, and that continues even now. This trend has brought the rate of population growth close to zero today in the West. The most puzzling of these puzzles is the behavior of family size, not the rate of technological improvement. Declining family size, I will argue, is a product of capitalism.

III

The decrease in family size that occurred during the nineteenth century is not a result of modern birth control techniques. Modern techniques had not yet made their appearance; and, in any case, people had been able to influence birth rates without modern techniques throughout much of human history. Timing of marriage and copulation and frequency of intercourse offered means of control. So did infanticide. The conquest of one people by another often led to the slaughtering of the conquered or to their relocation to places that did not support their continued survival. This relieved conquerors of the burdens of allocating food and other resources to the support of the conquered. Acquisition of these resources, after all, often motivated conquest. Less often, as during the Nazi reign in Western Europe, mass murder is motivated by a desire to rid society of persons who are convenient scapegoats, political threats, or whose presence is thought to be at odds with the culture of the dominant portion of the society.

More supportive of Malthus's theory would be reductions in child survival rates due to inadequate nutrition and disease, but, in fact, the opposite was true during and after the Industrial Revolution. The decline in family size occurred while economic conditions were improving. Smaller families also might result from cultural change. The displacement of Catholicism by Protestantism might lead to a reduction in family size, but quantitatively important conversion of this sort came well before the nineteenth century. One relevant change was an ongoing redistribution of population from rural areas to urban areas, but family size declined in both types of areas from the nineteenth century onward.

Some believe that growth in the fraction of people who are edu-
cated led to more emphasis on quality of child and less on quantity
of children. Perhaps, but education is not an exogenous consideration. It responds to more basic variables, including cultural changes,
and it is these variables, then, that are the source of decline in family size. Educational attainment surely is a function of wealth per
capita. This suggests that increases in wealth are responsible for
the decline in family size, but we lack a logical explanation of why
this should be so. In fact, through much of history, but not during contemporary times, urban wealthy families were larger than
families that were less wealthy. The explanation, it seems to me,
is not based on per capita wealth, but on how capitalism affected
the probability that wealth can be acquired and husbanded and the
manner in which it can be acquired.

Most people, throughout prehistory times and well into the
period of recorded history, did not expect to realize an increase in
their wealth during their lifetimes. Just prior to and during the
nineteenth century, this expectation changed because of mounting
evidence of an upward trend in material wealth, due mainly to
an earlier agricultural revolution followed by the Industrial Revolution. These institutions had many effects, of which two are
important to a release from Malthus's population trap – growing reliability of private ownership rights and growing reliance on
specialization in production.

Reliable privatization reinforced expectations that wealth
acquired through work, enterprise, and luck could be accumulated
without serious threat of theft or confiscation by others, including those higher up the hierarchical pyramid. This changed the
calculus that had previously guided behavior. The new calculus
raised the odds that a person could retain wealth and that wealth
could be increased during a person's lifetime. Accumulation of private wealth became a meaningful goal during the eighteenth and
nineteenth centuries.

Specialization in productive activities also became important during this period. This provided job opportunities away from home and it brought large numbers of laborers together in urban areas, many performing similar tasks. Where before, much labor was employed on the family farm or in artisan-like tasks in dispersed villages, it could now be employed in mills and factories where large numbers of persons were linked together in the performance or the similar kinds of work. Employment distant from the farm and village of one's birth loosened the hold parents had held over income earned by children and young adults. Specialization made it easier for laborers to unite in common cause.

The nuclear family, now that it could more reliably hold acquired wealth, would be inclined to make efforts to acquire more of it. It could do this in two ways, through work done by parents and work done by sons and daughters. Children, including here young adults, could acquire wealth for the family but only at the cost to the family of housing, feeding, and training them. The trade-offs, appropriately calculated, result in a preferred family size. This size was larger on the farm than in the city but, early on, it was not so much larger on the farm. Farm families employed their young on the family farm and in employment on neighboring farms. Urban families employed their young in the mills and factories that rose just before and during the Industrial Revolution. In both cases the parents exercised customary rights to the income received by their offspring. The maturing Industrial Revolution heightened forces that undermined much of parental control of the income of their children.

Mills and factories in towns and cities attracted young adult labor from rural areas and child labor from nearby urban neighborhoods. Farm parents no longer could rely as well or for as long on income from children as they aged. And it was in young adulthood that these children could bring in income that exceeded the cost they imposed on family. It now paid for farm families to gear down optimal family size and to adopt farming technologies that accommodated less labor input.

Adult laborers in mills and factories resisted the entry of child laborers. United in cause and united through organization within the mills, they succeeded in securing legislation that limited the use of child labor. Urban families, deprived of the opportunity for their children to earn income in mills, also reduced family size. Child labor legislation, however, never extended to farms. Children too young to leave the farm for city mills still offered a source of useful work for the family. One could argue, and people did argue, that (1) work on the farm was less debilitating to children than work in the mill and (2) work on the farm allowed children to remain closer to parents than did work in the mill. Accordingly, size of farm families, though it declined, did not decline as rapidly as did size of urban families.

The decline in the fraction of family income that parents could secure from children did not imply a decline in per capita wealth. The fraction of wealth transferred from control by parents to control by young adults did not reduce income per capita. To the extent that young adults are more productive when acting on their own behalf as compared to serving parents, per capita income will rise. And this surely was the case; if it were not, parents could have used financial incentives to keep young adults within the family fold. Per capita wealth rises while family size declines. Total population continued to increase as long as new family formation, increase in the survival rates of newborns, and longer life span outweighed reductions in family size. This was the case throughout most of the nineteenth and twentieth centuries. In recent decades, however, population growth has tapered off in the West and verges on turning negative. Part of the explanation for this is the opening of new career opportunities for women.

Capitalism's contribution to the breakout from Malthus's population trap was (1) to provide people with reliable rights to their income and savings, (2) to offer them opportunities to work at specialized tasks in mills and factories where they could be more productive, and (3) to make work conditions a place where labor could organize to pursue common goals and interests more effectively, as labor did in obtaining political restrictions against the use of child labor in mills, mines, and factories.

Child labor laws are a direct product of the state, and, in this case, of a state that had taken steps to provide for an electoral process, but the political muscle applied by adult labor to obtain this product was as much a product of capitalism, of its mills, mines, factories, and cities, as it was of the electoral process. The wisdom of child labor laws is not my concern here. My objective is to explain how people broke free from Malthus's population trap, a trap that, looking backward from Malthus's time, had held humanity in poverty for many thousands of years. Capitalism was involved in two ways: the upward trend in productivity it brought and the incentives it provided to keep family size in check. The reduction in family size that occurred is otherwise difficult to explain. Malthus probably would not have been so pessimistic about the future if capitalism had arrived several decades earlier.

In concluding this essay, I note that capitalism has only recently arrived in the Far East. This part of the world, until now at least, and unlike the West, has experienced continuing growth in total population. It may now, but it has not yet, escaped from Malthus's population trap. Consistent with what is said above, it also has failed to develop private property arrangements, relying instead on social arrangements that make parents depend on their children but that also give parents considerable control of the earnings of their children. In a collective sense, the advance of the welfare state in contemporary times in the West has created entitlement programs that have also made elderly persons, if not just parents, depend on income of the young, if not just children. And for reasons of democracy and demographics, the elderly have considerable say about the nature of these programs. However, population growth is not stimulated by these programs because those who live off the earnings of the young need not have brought these young into this world. The support base that is comprised of the young, therefore, will not grow as fast as it does in the Far East. A consequence of this may be collectively devised subsidies to those who bear children. These subsidies, if welfare entitlements programs remain in place, may yet put people of the West back into Malthus's population trap.

CAPITALISM AND ITS INSTITUTIONS

The end of the law is not to abolish or restrain, but to preserve and enlarge, freedom. For in all the states of created beings capable of laws, where there is no law there is no freedom. For liberty is to be free from restraint and violence from others; which cannot be where there is no law: and it is not, as we are told, a liberty for every man to do what he lists. (For who could be free when every other man's humour might domineer over him?) But a liberty to dispose, and order as he lists, his person, actions, possessions, and his whole property, within the allowance of those laws under which he is, and therein not to be the subject of the arbitrary will of another, but freely follow his own.

John Locke

5 THE LATE ARRIVAL OF CAPITALISM

C APITALISM IN THE FORM OF A BROADLY USED AND DURABLE
economic system did not become a fact until late in the nineteenth century. It has been with us for less than two centuries, a
very small percentage of the time that humans are known to have
existed. What took it so long to arrive?

I

Human activity during the greater part of mankind's history
was coordinated through collective or hierarchical organization
within groups containing relatively small numbers of people. These
groups competed with wolf packs and other predators but, since
they consumed vegetation as well as meat, they were able to specialize: women to tasks of gathering edible vegetation, preparing
food, and taking care of the young; men hunting and defending.
Contemporary work by paleontologists indicates that human population near the beginning of the Stone Age, about two and a
half million years ago, was small (Rogers, 1995) and was confined
largely to the African continent. Population began to fan out from
Africa to other parts of the world about 2 million years ago, reaching Europe about 500,000 years ago and Australia and the Americas much more recently. Toward the end of the Stone Age, from
50,000 to 10,000 years ago, human population increased rapidly. Up
until fairly recently, people experienced no significant trend-like

improvements in living conditions. Advantages that people gained from occasional improvements in the tools of hunting and improved knowledge about animals went mainly into population growth and not into sustained improvement in life. There is little reason to doubt that Malthus's population trap applied to human life for most of human existence. What seems true about hunter-gatherer life is that sufficient food was acquired to allow population to increase.

Many anthropologists have concluded, on the basis of studies of hunter-gatherer groups that still exist, that primitive people did not work full time at the tasks of gathering and hunting. There may be some bias downward in this calculation since the studies make no adjustment for time needed to get to sites with game and berries and to prepare food. Even so, primitive hunter-gatherers seemed to have free time. Some of this was used for leisure and propagation. The remainder seems to have been used in violent attacks on members of other groups. Existing hunter-gatherer groups tend to attack rival groups once a year, resulting in violent deaths that are a quarter of total deaths. Anthropologists interpret this violence in terms of a need to restrain population growth. I do not think this plausible interpretation gets to the root cause, which I attribute to the fact that game animals were freely available to all who would hunt. That is, much like the explanation of differences between Native Americans of the Northeast and Southwest with respect to land ownership, the nature-provided stock of edible animals was what I have called a communal good. This caused the population of these animals to dwindle relative to human needs. As a result, time and energy was given to the slaying of rival hunters. True, this might have made human population grow less rapidly, but, more to the point, because it reduced overhunting, it kept the stock of animals from declining as rapidly as it otherwise would have; it may also have increased the animal take per still-living person. Primitive groups were violent toward each other because they attempted to increase the kill realized by their own groups. There is considerable evidence that, despite these violent interactions, the nature-provided stock of choice animals diminished. A given amount of time and energy allocated to hunting ultimately resulted in less meat per capita. The Malthus population trap would close time and again after each improvement in hunting technique.[1]

As is true today for most nonhuman creatures, human survival during primitive times depended very much on perishables (although the smoking of meat and exposure to cold weather could lengthen the usable period). Moreover, to be successful hunters and foragers, these small groups of people needed to remain on the move, since a given site can be quickly stripped of edible plants and game. Human backs and stomachs, perhaps aided by some drag poles, limited the load-carrying capacity of a primitive group. Food and other goods in quantities that exceeded what people could carry would have been redundant. This lifestyle not only ruled out amassing large quantities of food but also the accumulating of physical assets. Bringing down a very large tree would serve no purpose, since it could not be transported easily nor could it be of use on the spot, since the group would soon need to move.

The important consequence of this lifestyle, then, is that it made accumulation of material wealth impractical and it kept nutrition close to subsistence. Yet, to abandon this lifestyle would have been disastrous. Like other pack predatory animals, humans were locked into a way of living that maintained life but undermined improvement in life. The only product of this life is population expansion, mainly achieved by dramatic moves to parts of the world that were not yet overhunted, but also by improvement in weapons. Humans were better at this life than were other pack hunters, so human population increased relative to the population of their rivals. Even so, Malthus's population trap repeatedly closed on humans.

---

[1] The addendum to this essay briefly reviews "Toward a Theory of Property Rights," the article referred to here, but it does so in order to show the need for revision. This need becomes apparent for reasons the present essay will make clear.

Population growth might have encouraged group territoriality. A large enough group might have effectively policed a territory large enough to allow a "reservoir" that held a continuing supply of prey; food taken from this reservoir could be taken to a "home base" within it. If and when this became true, the group, tribe, or clan would have begun to displace small-group organization, but this outcome is unlikely because one square mile of land seems to be needed to support one person if the group lives by hunting and foraging. If many other equally good territories are available, why use human and other resources to defend a fixed large territory?

The imperatives of this lifestyle argued in favor of group collectivism, since teamwork was essential to obtain sufficient food. Food was probably shared as a result. There was little opportunity for anything like "precapitalism" to arise. Neither food nor other assets could be amassed by individuals or even by the team. Capitalism awaited a basic change in the food acquisition system. This came, of course, with farming, a way of earning a living that, after farming became productive, offered storable, transportable food without demanding high mobility of the producers of this food. The essential consequence of this was to make private ownership practical. Constant movement could be avoided and grains were storable, so, at last, it would become possible to accumulate wealth by privatization of land ownership.

II

The turn to agriculture seems to have begun between nine thousand and twelve thousand years ago, the time slot during which anthropologists find the first evidence of primitive farming of seeds not observed during earlier times. A few sites dispersed across the world show this evidence, but anthropologists are not sure if primitive farming became possible because of changed climatic conditions or pressures emanating from shortages of normally consumed foods. I believe that shortages played a key role, even if climate and luck were also at work. There is plenty of evidence that rival groups of people, with free access to prey and slight improvements in weapons, were gradually reducing the supply of edible animals. The pressure for change in human organization must have become more intense than when migration to distant lands was easy. We may take this period in human history as the launching point for a food acquisition revolution; a revolution that made private ownership of resources much more practical.

Although farming would eventually allow people to survive with an immobile lifestyle, the earliest farmers, like hunter-gatherers, could not long remain in one location because land fertility diminished quickly. After a year or two of farming a plot of land, people would need to abandon it in favor of virgin land. Slash-and-burn technology was used to clear forestland. The food produced on any one farm probably did not exceed by much the needs of those who did the farming. Technical change, including new strategies for using land, ultimately changed this, but very slowly. The earliest use of a hand-drawn plough that has been discovered dates this tool at about four thousand years ago. Irrigation ditches make their appearance five hundred years later. Three-field farming systems emerged much later. This involved rotation of different sections of a farm, in which one section is used to graze stock, which adds natural fertilizer to the soil while it is being grazed. A second section is used to grow legumes, which restores nitrogen to the soil, and a third section is used to grow grain. This substituted for a two-field system that had divided land into crop growing and animal pasturing. As these changes occurred, it became increasingly possible for farmers to remain in one location for long periods. The later use of fertilizer extended this time period indefinitely. Field rotation and use of manure took place as early as the fourteenth century in small regions of Europe, such as around Flanders, but widespread use of manure on privately enclosed (not collectively controlled) fields in England awaited the eighteenth century. The technical development of the reaper and binder ended a production bottleneck whose source was the labor-intensive harvesting of crops. The later mechanization of farms extended this revolution well into the nineteenth century.

The spread of farming and successive improvements in farm productivity had important effects, four of which may be mentioned: (1) the need for mobility was reduced; (2) important farm products, such as grain and legumes, could be stored without rapid degradation; (3) private enclosure of collective strip farms became more rewarding; and (4) new legal arrangements emerged to facilitate effective control of land by private owners and to establish secure arrangements for the exchange of "excess" farm produce for "excess" goods of other types.

Reduction in the need for mobility meant that asset accumulation could take place more easily. The main assets were land and the quantities of foodstuffs that could be grown, stored, and shipped. Later came new tools and equipment. The constraints that hunter-gatherer life had imposed on people became less important. For the first time in human history it became possible for many people to enjoy an above-subsistence living standard if farm productivity could improve faster than population.

Privatization of agricultural land began to occur most quickly in England, where private enclosures began to replace collectively controlled strip farms. The collective farm entitled each farm villager to the produce of randomly distributed strips of farmland. The random distribution of strips helped to ensure a fair draw on crop production by diversifying the risk of holding land of poor quality, poor drainage, and susceptibility to insect infestation. However, choosing which crops to plant and techniques of land management to use were hampered by cumbersome collective decision-making procedures and by the risk-averseness of villagers. Risk-avoiding psychology is evidenced by the long-held preference for strip farming. Old ways were clung to strongly. If each villager were to be allowed to go his or her own way with respect to the strips allocated to him, there would arise a costly lack of uniformity in the uses to which these separately controlled strips were put, making it difficult to have a general plan for harvesting, field rotation, and use of innovative techniques and technical developments. Hence, this "equitable" or "insurance" form of farm organization stood as an obstacle to innovative use of land and to the abandonment of strip farming by the village collectives to whom the land belonged. Enclosures in England were accomplished at first through voluntarily arranged buyouts of the collective farmlands, especially during the eighteenth century; the increased frequency of buyouts gives evidence of private wealth accumulation. Later, during the early part of the nineteenth century, enclosures were coerced into existence by appeals made to Parliament for measures that made it more difficult for farming to remain collectivized.

Successful enclosure demanded revenues that were expected to exceed costs of acquiring and policing land, so the pace of enclosure correlated with market prices for crops. The division of gains to be won from voluntarily arranged enclosures was determined through negotiation between buyers of collective farmland and collectively acting sellers of this land, but higher crop prices made for a larger total gain. In this manner, but sometimes through intervention by the state, private ownership of rural lands substituted for collective ownership. This, in turn, accelerated the adoption of new, productive techniques of farming.

Enclosure of open fields was only one of many kinds of change that, together, resulted in a private ownership economy. Changes in law modified land inheritance customs and made it easier for land title to be transferred between private parties. Inheritance, it should be noticed, is of little value in the mobile lifestyle of hunter-gatherers, but farm life, especially after innovations of one sort or another, allowed the same parcel of land to be used for decades and, eventually, "forever." The legal system conferred durable, alienable ownership rights on users of durable land sites. Exchange of assets became more important, and, in response, legal arrangements were altered to make exchange easier and surer. Sir

Henry Maine, the famous English historian, in his *Ancient Law* (1861, pp. 168–9), describes the transformation taking place during the eighteenth and nineteenth centuries as follows:

[I]t has been distinguished by the gradual dissolution of family dependency, and the growth of individual obligation in its place. The Individual is steadily substituted for the Family, as the unit of which civil laws take account . . . it [is not] difficult to see what is the tie between man and man which replaces by degrees those forms of reciprocity in rights and duties which have their origin in the Family. It is Contract. [F]rom a condition of society in which all the relations of Persons are summed up in the relations of Family, we seem to have steadily moved towards a phase of social order in which all these relations arise from the free agreement of Individuals.[2]

Although sometimes interrupted by periods of contrary movement, the transformation to private ownership began first and went furthest in Holland and Britain. The Dutch and English tradition of trading overseas may have had something to do with their early start; it prepared for dealing with strangers, a consideration, as I argue below, that is precondition to a transition to capitalism. The strong landed aristocracy, representing farming interests, limited the power of the British Crown. Reliance on common-law legal procedures made law responsive to changes that sprang from new ways to use resources. Whatever the sources, Britain followed Holland in coming early to a system that supported private ownership and regular exchange of entitlements, thus establishing necessary conditions for capitalism to arise.

---

[2] According to Lal (2006) and Berman (1983) the seeds for the trend toward privatization and contract were sowed during the eleventh century by Pope Gregory VII who, in attempting to encourage an inflow of funds into a financially strained Catholic Church, issued edicts that called for respect of merchants, for honoring of contracts, and for the freedom of individuals from family and collective control of their funds. This not only encouraged a flow of funds to the church from widows who by law and custom would need to conserve their estates and pass them to offspring and other relatives, but it also helped change social attitudes toward commercial activities.

III

The technical, legal, and organizational changes just described were sparked by the change in natural endowments wrought by the appearance of farmable grasses. Ultimately, this led to a different lifestyle and to wealth accumulation. Importantly, it also made human society much more dependent on specialization of productive activities. Heightened specialization made it possible to produce food, especially food such as grain that can be stored, in excess of the survival needs of those who worked the farms. The excess could be stored and shipped to nonfarmers. Whereas hunter-gatherer life required the engagement of most people in hunting and foraging, farming permitted many people, and, ultimately, a very large fraction of population, to work in nonfarming activities.

"Excess" farm product sustained nonfarm work of various kinds. Unlike hunter-gatherer life, these excesses allowed for mutually beneficial exchanges between a variety of specialists, including farmers. Specialists in farming provided foodstuffs to support other specialists engaged in mining, smelting, lumbering, and shipping, and these provided materials, supplies, and machinery to farming specialists, and so on. All these activities reflected the absence of any necessity to live a mobile lifestyle; goods moved more, people moved less. Specialization became much more important than it possibly could have been in the Stone Age or in the age of primitive farming. Western countries had entered the stage of specialization (but had not yet fully entered the stage of scale-favoring specialization).

An imperative of all this was that trade took place increasingly between persons who were unrelated, who were not members of the same small group or clan, and who, essentially, were strangers who often were located in different regions. Rights and obligations that give security to strangers who deal with each other became necessary. These developments in law and custom made scale-favoring technical change more promising, for large scale requires that goods be sold to many persons who are strangers to those who produce these goods. Industrialization, even more than farming, involved production in quantities greatly in excess of the needs of those whose work produced this production. The consequences of this are profound. If gains from specialization are to be won, people need to become comfortable and secure in their dealings with others who, for the most part, are strangers.

The stage for industrialization was set in place during the sixteenth century in Britain, when the government sought to improve the cannons it planned to install on the naval fleet then being created. The old-style cannons were made of forged iron; they had limited range and they were prone to explode if the charge installed was on the high side. Bronze cannons were better, but were costly. The English turned to cast iron and created facilities to cast naval cannons. These facilities stood ready to be joined to supplies of coal and steam engines during the eighteenth century. The seventeenth century and the "Glorious" Revolution stood in the interval between these two events. Catholic King James II was removed from the British throne and replaced with his Protestant nephew and son-in-law King William III. The consequences were quite important, not only for Britain but also, later, for the American Revolution. English law and governance were changed in ways that advanced representative government, law, and individual freedom. These changes, together with cast iron, coal, and steam engines, launched the Industrial Revolution late in the eighteenth century. Within fifty to seventy-five years of this beginning, England became an industrial economy. Mass production undermined not only institutions geared to small scale but also old customs that favored self-sufficiency and personalized dealings. The feudal village and, later, the isolated peasant farm gave way to commerce, and commerce increasingly became dependent on extensive specialization. These are not chance happenings. There would have been no demand for or benefit from them in societies based on hunting and foraging; and they could not be made very useful within cultures that valued isolation and self-sufficiency. They made sense only if scale could be used to serve masses of people who were largely unknown to each other. The gradual improvements in farm productivity, the increase in population and its relocation in towns and cities, and the displacement of collectivism by private ownership created the possibility of recovering the larger up-front costs required by large-scale production. The setting that gradually came into place offered large markets to those who could serve them. Technical changes made it possible to serve these markets at low costs. Growing density of population and changing legal systems made dealings between strangers more acceptable and reliable. People who were unknown to each other and to owners of firms were increasingly willing to accept lower prices in compensation for dealing with strangers or with institutions in which strangers worked.

Once industrialization began to take hold, there ensued a transformation to "full" industrialization that was so rapid that it could have been witnessed within a person's lifetime. The culture of self-sufficiency and isolation, of dependency on kin and neighbors, and of reliance on reciprocation and collective decisions had been completely displaced seventy-five years after serious industrialization began. What emerged was an economy built on specialization and a people who were willing to engage in exchange with those not personally known to them. Marx later made much of what he called the separation of the worker from his product and of the inability of people to consult only themselves in choosing a lifestyle. This essentially depicts strangers interacting with strangers because of the gains to be had from specialization. Indeed, workers might feel less in control of their lives in this new economy, but its main consequence was not worker powerlessness but a future, perhaps to be realized a generation or two later, in which ordinary persons could realize the comforts of greater personal wealth, a more interesting life, and a view of their children's future that shone even more brightly. None of this was possible throughout most of human history.

It would be rare indeed if so large a gain were to be unaccompanied by some sacrifice. Most people making a careful judgment about this new lifestyle will judge the gain worth the cost. There is no denying that capitalism brought material progress to people on a scale never before experienced. From 1800 to 2000, for example, global life expectancy at birth rose from about thirty years to sixty-seven years, and in countries of the West it rose to more than seventy-five. The lengthening of life span could not have happened without material progress, for this helped to improve not just medical science but also nutrition, water supply, sanitation, and housing. In the United States, real incomes now are more than twice what they were in 1960, and by 1960 they had already climbed far from levels enjoyed a century earlier. Three-quarters of families in the United States own their own homes, compared with one-fifth a century ago. The size of the average house in the United States is twice the size it was a quarter-century ago. Air and water are cleaner. And, contrary to the inverse relationship between population and per capita wealth posited by Malthus, there has been a positive correlation between population and material progress.

About 80 percent of the population of developed countries worked farms at the beginning of the nineteenth century; throughout the rest of the world this percentage was greater than 90 percent. From 1300 to 1800, the percentage of people living in urban areas in Europe increased only a bit, from 10.4 to 12.1. Life expectancy and caloric intake had remained at fairly constant levels throughout most of human history. It was not until the seventeenth century that life expectancy in Britain reached levels slightly above the twenty-five years that is estimated to have been the expected life span of citizens of the Roman Empire almost two thousand years earlier. European population grew from the first century A.D., but only slowly until 1700, when, from 1750 to 1800, population increased by 50 percent. It was during the last half of the eighteenth century that agricultural productivity in Britain began to trend upward, and did so more steeply during the nineteenth century as new machinery began to be applied to farming. The fraction of people engaged in farming then began its steady decline, falling to levels today that are astonishingly low. And all the while this was happening, per capita wealth also increased. We're not talking "peanuts" here, but extraordinary progress.

Scale-favoring specialization quickly transformed an economy that already had become mostly privatized into one built on private ownership plus extensive specialization. Such an economy involves investment in and construction of assets that are durable and whose values are dependent on the use of assets owned by others. This puts owners of resources at risk of appropriation by marauders and others. This risk is of minor consequence in hunter-forager-scavenger life, which involves "hand-to-mouth" living and demands very little "up-front" investment, but it is of major consequence if scale-favoring specialization is to yield its bountiful product. Necessary to the making of these investments are laws that protect rights of ownership and maintain order.

Collective control of resources works well enough if group size is small and necessary decisions are few, but it becomes impractical in the presence of extensive specialization. Specialization is based on multiple decisions by people familiar with the particular conditions of their specializations and it requires a practical method for adjusting quickly to changes that take place in the interfaces that link these specializations. Decentralization and private ownership are the practical answers when productivity growth requires scale-favoring specialization. The centrally planned economy, which is to be distinguished from a truly collective economy, and which is more hierarchically organized, is incapable of dealing with an economy in which there exists a complex mixture of specialized activities. This is largely for the same reasons that make collectivism impractical. However, economic theory for the analysis of markets, prices, and decentralized organization does not provide an understanding of how, or how well, collective groups or planning bureaucracies tackle resource allocation problems. Economic theory provides an understanding of how a decentralized, private ownership economy resolves the puzzle of spontaneous order, but it does not provide an understanding of the ways in which institutional arrangements that differ from the decentralized economic system resolve resource allocation problems. The claim that these alternative institutional arrangements fail to resolve these problems as well as does the decentralized economic system is supported mainly by the facts and experiences provided during the last half-century. It seems from this history that material progress achieved in economic systems that significantly limit the role played by central planning cannot be matched by those that do not.

This is so even on an examination of more recent times. Shortly before World War II and continuing to the present, Western Europe's industrialized countries have relied on policies that soften what they perceive to be the effects of capitalism, providing extensive social support in matters involving health, labor involvement in business policy, and other such concerns. The United States, although presently seeking to do some softening of its own, has held to policies that are more tolerant of market outcomes. Real per capita GDP in the United States is more than 15 percent greater than in the richest of the West European countries. The U.S. unemployment rate has generally been significantly lower than these countries', and, despite some increase in income inequality in recent years in the United States, inequality is still greater across Western Europe. This somewhat surprising fact is no doubt attributable to policies in Western Europe that, in attempting to soften market outcomes, subsidize people in ways that allow them, without much work and risk-taking, to have a minimally acceptable standard of living; as a result, as a fraction of population, more people in Western Europe live at this minimally acceptable level than is true for the United States.

So, of what do critics of capitalism now complain? That Americans work too hard. This may or may not be, depending on the criterion that is used to measure "too hard." Americans choose to work, however, whereas many Western Europeans are forced by law or seduced by subsidies to do less work. This suggests one more important precondition for material progress. This is a broad-based human desire to be materially better off. While we are disposed to want time for rest and contemplation, and while children are inclined to think that rabbits and squirrels have great lives, most adults are acquisitive enough to seek material progress, and they do so even at the cost of working hard and taking risks.

IV

The trend toward private ownership became visible in Mesopotamia, stronger in the Greek city-states, and still stronger in the Roman Empire, whose laws governing ownership and exchange were precedent setting. The fall of Rome in the West marked the first major disruption of what had been a steplike transformation toward capitalism. It was followed by 500 years of Dark Ages and, later, by the emergence of church and feudal institutions, all of which were hardly reflective of capitalism. Security was sought through isolation and self-sufficiency except in major cities, such as existed in northern Italy and the Lowlands. Isolation and self-sufficiency are hardly congenial to capitalism, but cities and city-states gradually became stronger, and so did trade across large distances. The institutions of capitalism retrenched and grew in importance as feudalism retreated and nation-states advanced. This movement toward institutions of capitalism became still stronger during the sixteenth and seventeenth centuries and, finally, attained a point of maturity midway into the nineteenth century. The free trade aspect of this maturity began and then weakened during the last half of the nineteenth century, but other aspects of capitalism remained strong.

The second major disruption in the development of capitalism was marked by a shift from capitalism to central planning. It began in Germany before World War I, accelerated with the Russian revolution in 1917, continued during the 1930s Depression, and extended its reach in the aftermath of World War II. The abandonment of institutions of capitalism was deliberate in the Soviet Union. The weakening of capitalism in the West was not entirely an accident of the Great Depression. President Roosevelt adopted policies in the United States during the decade of the 1930s that launched a variety of programs designed to substitute state planning and state-sponsored collusion for open markets. These programs, which included substantial tariff barriers to international trade, were put into place as remedies for the Depression, but they undoubtedly lengthened and made it more severe. Socialism marched onward from one world catastrophe to another. Its scope increased after each major catastrophe, World War I, the Great Depression, and World War II, and reached a pinnacle of success following the end of World War II.

Central planning of a sort that is identified with communism and socialism proved incapable of matching the economic progress that continued to deliver material progress to large numbers of people in those economies that have retained strong components of capitalism. A quarter-century after World War II, the trend toward market-based economies returned and, to date, has seriously reduced the reach and intensity of socialism in Eastern Europe and the Far East. The failure of central planning is due in part to the complexity of economies based on extensive specialization. What can be planned and controlled adequately in a kin group or comparatively small community is largely beyond control in a large economy based on extensive specialization. However, the testing of capitalism is likely to continue, not because it will fail to deliver material progress, but because of repeated attempts to use the political arena to modify the market-produced distribution of wealth. It is not yet clear if modification has proceeded to the point of undermining capitalism or, given the dissatisfaction of some with capitalism, if a degree of modification is essential to maintain popular political support for this engine of material progress.

v

Throughout this essay I have used "capitalism" without pausing to define exactly what I mean. Why burden the reader and disrupt the flow of the explanation if the reader has a pretty good idea of what capitalism means? So, I have waited for the end of this essay to clarify what I mean.

Capitalism is an economy based on decentralized private owner-ship of resources and open markets; "based on" means that private ownership rights are acknowledged and respected. Most members of society must feel a duty to respect the private rights of others. Ownership rights must be exercisable without fear, ridicule, or dis-respect from other members of society. An economic system that is forced on people will not perform as would one to which there is general assent.

Even with this added condition, we have not yet touched all essential elements of capitalism. The word "capitalism" was put into our vocabulary by followers of Karl Marx because he meant something more than a decentralized private ownership economy. He referred to accumulation of large pools of capital in private hands, noting that these allowed privately acting individuals to undertake tasks that earlier would be undertaken by the state or the community. He complained that things had reached a stage at which privately acting individuals could displace the community in the performance of tasks that, on a collective basis, had been under-taken on behalf of the entire community. Now, with capitalism, they were being undertaken on behalf of private parties. I do not intend to pause to argue with Marx's concern by pointing to the invisible hand that Smith had seen as marshaling private efforts to serve the public good. I do, however, sense that Marx had a notion of capitalism that is not to be swept aside.

Capitalism, when properly viewed as a substitute for state control of resources, waits upon the accumulation of large sums of private wealth before it can serve this view. This may happen through the accumulation of large sums in private hands or it may happen through the development of capital markets that, at costs lower than the tax system (including here the value of personal freedom), can marshal capital from decentralized private owners of smaller sums of capital. Since capitalism substitutes private means for centrally controlled or communally controlled means, its existence requires either the accumulation of large sums in private hands or the development of markets though which smaller sums can be exchanged and accumulated voluntarily. These conditions were not widely met until late in the seventeenth and early in the eighteenth centuries in England.

APPENDIX: ON THE THEORY OF
PRIVATE OWNERSHIP

M AINSTREAM ECONOMISTS, DURING THE NINETEENTH AND early part of the twentieth century gave considerable attention to the price system but not to the underlying property right system on which the price system rests in a capitalist economy. So, economists were surprised when R. H. Coase (1959) claimed, in an article on the Federal Communication Commission, that the FCC is unnecessary to avoid interference between broadcasters in the uses they make of frequency signals. He wrote:

A private-enterprise system cannot function properly unless property rights are created in resources, and, when this is done, someone wishing to use a resource has to pay the owner to obtain it. Chaos disappears; and so does the government except that a legal system to define property rights and to arbitrate disputes is, of course, necessary. (p. 14)

The interference that concerned supporters of FCC regulation is in the nature of an externality, and, so, Coase's claim, if correct, implied rejection or at least revision of the externality doctrine that had by that time become accepted doctrine in economics. He was called upon to defend this implication, and he did this in his classic 1960 article on "The Problem of Social Cost." In that article, Coase examines the consequences of alternative assignments of ownership rights. He asks readers to compare the consequences for resource allocation of giving farmers the right to graze their cattle without being liable for damages done to a neighboring farmer's crops by cattle that accidentally stray from the path on which they are being led to the consequences that would follow if, instead, the farmer enjoyed a right to grow crops unmolested by the rancher's cattle. His well-known conclusion is that there would be no difference in resource allocation if farmer and rancher could freely negotiate with each other but that there would be a difference if there were positive costs of negotiation. Coase's purpose, however, was to examine the externality problem and not the private ownership system itself. In effect, he assumed the existence of a private ownership system.[3]

Seven years later, stimulated by his work, I discussed conditions that would cause private ownership to emerge from a system in which resources were collectively or communally owned (Demsetz, 1967). The preceding essay in this chapter, in its discussion of the late arrival of capitalism, suggests that these conditions have a broader field of application and also that other conditions are involved. I bring these conditions up to date in this addendum. What I will say here is best grasped if the reader understands the essentials of my 1967 article, and so, with apologies to readers familiar with that article, I begin with a brief summary of its main argument.

The literary "hook" in the article was an anthropological puzzle concerning property rights to land among Native American tribes. As the seventeenth century came to an end, the status of land control along the eastern part of the border that would later separate Canada and the United States underwent a transformation. Tribal-based collective ownership gave way to family-based private ownership. Why had this change taken place? And why did it not take place on Native American lands located on the Great Plains and in the American Southwest?

---

[3] Later essays on externalities and on the firm will raise objections to Coase's conclusions about the implications of transaction cost. At the time my 1967 article on property rights was written, I accepted the notion that externalities result from positive cost of transacting, including the costs of transacting between present and future generations.

Appendix: On the Theory of Private Ownership

The resolution I offered was based on two aspects of the situation: the development of the European fur trade and the difference between forest and grazing animals in land-use habits. The growing fur trade resulted in increases in fur prices and in the scale of hunting. Both considerations increased the loss that would result from hunting on collectively controlled land. These losses arose because a trapper had no great personal interest in curtailing his take of furs by setting fewer traps so that a larger stock of living animals would be able to propagate, since no part of the resulting future stock of animals belonged to him. Overhunting today meant that trapping efforts tomorrow would yield fewer furs, but this cost was in the nature of an externality born mainly by others in the future. The Native American tribes located in the region, however, did have an interest in the future. Private family ownership was allowed to replace collective ownership. This reduced the severity of the problem because the nature of forest animals is to remain close to their dens. A family that owned land could keep others from trapping animals on it and would have an incentive to do so because it retained control of (most of) the future stock of animals, something that would not have been true under a communal ownership arrangement. The same pressures must have been felt in the American Southwest, but the grazing animals that populated the southwestern plains strayed far and wide, and so, privatization of land ownership in the Southwest would not have created effective control of present or future stocks of grazing animals. Hence, land rights were not privatized but, instead, remained in communal form with the nations or tribes of Native Americans that populated the Southwest.

I attributed the transformation of land ownership in the Northeast to the fact that the European fur trade had raised the value that was lost through the communal ownership arrangement in the Northeast. This strengthened incentives to alter land ownership arrangements and led Native Americans in this region to accept family-based private ownership of land.

This logic offered at least the beginning of a theory of changes in ownership rights. The European fur trade created incentives to privatize land in the north, but if the behavior of fur bearing animals in the North somehow experienced a change in their food acquisition strategies such that they adopted the roaming tactics of fur bearing animals of the Southwest, then, since costs are incurred to maintain private rights, it could well be that communal ownership would become the efficient form of ownership. The theory explains changes in ownership arrangements, not just the emergence of private ownership. Privatization of land holdings in combination with the natural habits of forest animals made for a practical solution to the problem actually faced by Native Americans in the North. The efficient solution for land ownership in the Southwest was communal ownership, not private ownership. This would not change until barbed wire made it practical to fence in farm land and keep roaming cattle off some tracts of land.

The discussion of the late arrival of capitalism leads me to believe that what I wrote in 1967 only opens the door to what could be a more full-blown theory of private property rights. The argument I employed in that paper begins with the observation that expansion in the European fur trade increased the loss being suffered as a result of overhunting. This helps to explain not only why Native Americans of the Northeast allowed privatization of land to take place, but also explains why, for centuries earlier, they did not. The Native American population was too small to overtax the available supply of fur-bearing animals.

The essay applies the same logic to primitive groups, all of which had free access to hunt edible animals. Overhunting occurred, and, as one would expect, was accompanied by the killing of hunters from rival groups, since it was not possible to privatize ownership of animals or of meat, given the constraints of a mobile lifestyle of hunter-gatherers. Farming ultimately ended reliance on mobile living, and control of land directly conveyed control of crops. The incentives to engage in farming reflected the increasing difficulty faced by a growing population of people who were busy destroying the sources of their meat.

Why not generalize from this to formulate explanations about the long-term trend toward privatization in the world? Population has steadily increased throughout most of the world. Only in recent decades has the rate of growth in population diminished in the most economically developed countries. One can extend the argument about privatization of land by Native Americans, which relies on growth in the European fur trade, to the increasing value of food in a world in which population steadily grows. This growth, plus the diminishing stock of animals, steadily raises the externality cost associated with hunter life. Assume there is a "natural" preference for communal arrangements that is indulged only as long as the cost of doing so is not great. Such arrangements, after all, were prevalent and dominant throughout most of human history. As population increases, the waste entailed in external costs that emanate from overhunting becomes more important and more worth reducing. The effect of population growth extends, of course, to expressway congestion and central city congestion. Add population growth as a condition that generally, but perhaps not always, makes externality problems more worth reducing.

A second line of development would set aside the externality problem and turn to the wealth distribution problem. The involuntary taking of wealth diminishes incentives to create wealth. The easier it is to engage in what we might consider "theft" and the greater the amount of wealth that might be taken involuntarily, the greater is the wealth that is threatened by theft, the more serious will be the incentive effects of theft, and the more willing people will be to invest in discouraging thieves. The Industrial Revolution made the theft problem more serious. It ushered in a reorganization of production based on large up-front investment in plant and equipment. This reduced the use of dispersed family units of production that characterized the putting-out system. The centralization of production in mills and factories created rich, immobile targets, not only for thieves but also for angry mobs. As compared with the dispersed production arrangements used in the putting-out system, which offered a degree of "portfolio" diversification, the Industrial Revolution raised the level of risk per unit of assets or per unit of wealth. Full realization of the advantages of industrialization required preservation of incentives to invest, and this, in turn, required greater clarity of, and more protection for, private ownership rights.

In addition, but certainly not less important, industrialization rested on specialization of production in which goods are produced by a few and made available for sale to the many. Theft and destruction of plant and equipment threatened the well-being of more would-be users of goods because they no longer possessed quickly marshaled capabilities to engage in self-sufficient production. One need only look at the consequences today at what would happen to the supply of gasoline and to its price should there be a successful terrorist attack on a large Middle East refinery. No similarly severe disruption would have been possible in a world that relied on wood-burning fires. The specialization of production, in which a few centers of production serve many millions of persons, threatens to undermine incentives to invest unless meaningful rights to exclusive use of productive assets are put into place. To a lesser degree, the same specialization, calling forth the same consequences, occurs when hunter-gatherer life is reduced in favor of a farm-based food supply system. Farming creates an inventory of durable food supplies held in fixed locations, whereas hunting-gathering minimizes the amount of foods that are stored. Farms thus offer richer targets for thieves and invading armies than did the one-time connection between food acquisition and food consumption during primitive times.

I am suggesting that changes taking place through long periods of time, and that took place more quickly through the eighteenth and nineteenth centuries, raised the social payoff from curtailing theft, mob violence, and marauding. Enforced private rights of ownership offered a way to do this. Of course, the state could have become the creator and owner of assets as these changes took place, and, in fact, it has threatened doing so. But central planning is a form of collectivism that has failed to achieve the productive results that have been obtained through the personalized incentives created by a private ownership system. As a result, despite the contest between these two systems, the net effects of growth in population, in scale, in immobility of production unit, and in specialization have worked in favor of a private ownership rights system.

6 OWNERSHIP AND EXCHANGE

T HE MAIN BODY OF THE PRESENT ESSAY CONSISTS OF A GENERAL discussion of ownership, noting some of the complications involved in attempting to give clarity to the concept of ownership. I return to this topic in the essay on the public corporation, where, among several other issues, is that of "Who owns the corporation?" The last part of this essay gives an explanation of the work of R. H. Coase when he discusses a hypothetical world in which it cost nothing to use the price system. This discussion is included here to prepare readers unfamiliar with Coase's work for Essay 7.

I

Markets and the price system lie at the center of economic theory, but they rest on an institution that this theory hardly touches: private ownership of resources. If people create markets in which they expect to exchange assets, they must have title to these assets. Ownership entitlement is simply presumed in much of what we call economic theory. This often is true even in discussions in which ownership is explicitly discussed. R. H. Coase, whose ideas are discussed below and in the next essay, discusses the difference, if any, in the uses made of resources if the identities of the persons who own these resources are "shuffled" in hypothetical comparisons. His discussion of this issue explicitly involves ownership. Yet, it takes the existence and nature of a private ownership system as a known given. The issue he raises would make no sense if ownership were not already an operable institutional arrangement.

Thus, there are two components to the social arrangement used to resolve competing interests in a market-based economy. One is the institution of private ownership; the second is a legal system that makes exchange of owned assets a reliable activity. Out of this come markets that resolve differences in the way people would like scarce resources to be used.

Ownership may be treated as a simple concept for heuristic purposes when discussing theory, but it is not at all simple. The complexities of ownership are illustrated in Herman Melville's classic, *Moby Dick*. He notes that whalers who worked the East Coast whaling grounds trade and who had successfully harpooned a whale and secured it to their whaling ship had established a right of ownership in the whale. If they fail to make it "fast" to their ship, however, or if the whale comes "loose" once made fast, other whalers can take possession of the whale and make it fast to their ship; if successful in doing this, the second acquirer of the whale becomes its owner. Melville tells us the practice was not codified in U.S. or state laws but, rather, in and by the practice of East Coast whalers. He frames this practice as being in accord with two rules: (1) A Fast-Fish belongs to the party fast to it. (2) A Loose-Fish is fair game for anybody who soonest can catch it. Melville then suggests some of the complexities that might arise when attempting to apply these rules. Do they apply equally to live and dead fish? In what manner must the fish be made fast to the whaler? By a cable? A mast? An oar? And so on. It is easy to see that clear resolution of ownership rights is no easy matter.

Setting aside the potential conflicts that might arise between whalers in the future, this example reveals one important way in which ownership of a scarce resource comes about. The whale becomes owned when it comes under human control. Environmentalists have claimed that the whale owns itself, much as a person who is a citizen of a free society is free from involuntarily imposed controls (imposed by others). These environmentalists view the capture of the whale much as a free people would view the enslavement of an African native. And, just as most people see injustice in human slavery, so some environmentalists see injustice in the taking of a whale and depriving it of freedom of movement and even of life. I see nothing wrong in their position, although I may disagree with it.

My objection is to the terminology often used by environmentalists. The history of ownership discusses ownership as a relationship between people in the uses they make of resources. It does not relate to animals and plants in the sense of describing how they interact in the uses they make of resources. Nor does it describe how a plant or an animal may use people.

As an institutional achievement of civilization, the meaning of ownership merits respect. As a concept, ownership applies to people who interact in a social setting. There is no operational content to an animal or plant owning itself. A restriction on the logging of redwood trees is a restriction imposed by people on other people who are owners of redwood trees. It is correctly described as a restriction on private ownership, as a regulation of human behavior, and is only confusingly thought of as freeing redwood trees from a condition of slavery. How would a redwood exercise freedom? Have you ever walked up to a tree and inquired of it just how much (or whether) it wants to part with a few bushels of the nuts that form part of it? Or how much it wants to allow people to use the shade it casts? Or how much it wants to be transformed in building lumber? The tree has no capability for responding to such offers, nor can it make offers of its own in an attempt to acquire resources from people (or from other trees). What does the tree want to do with itself? How do environmentalists know it wants to remain standing on a damp, dreary West Coast slope? Try asking it. *You* want the tree to remain where it is? Fine. But let us not pretend this makes the tree an owner of itself. Private ownership as a social convention determines which people *exercise control of scarce resources and how they may interact when using these resources,* including whales and trees; it does not determine which animals and vegetables exercise control over people.

Environmentalists can use resources they own in a manner that is consistent with their beliefs. This includes using their resources to secure legislation that regulates the uses that other people may make of resources. Legislation that bars people from logging redwood trees may result, but let us not confuse this with a claim that the trees own themselves or that they decide for themselves how they shall be used. After all, legislators and citizen-petitioners of legislators are people. It is they, not the trees, who seek and acquire legislation.

II

And how do people acquire ownership rights? Well, in many ways. Some 500,000 years ago, our ancestors began to migrate from Africa to Europe. The new land they occupied was, so to speak, "caught" by them when they set foot on it and defended their use of it, something like the way Melville's whalers acquired rights in a whale. Taking possession of a resource that is unclaimed has played an important role in establishing ownership rights through much of the early history of humans. Once such rights are established in a social system that relies on private ownership of resources, ownership is changed through voluntarily given agreement. Usually, this involves an exchange of assets. War, coercion, theft, and fraud are other ways of acquiring the already-owned resources of others, but these methods, although they certainly have been used, reflect interaction between two societies, at least one of which does not accept the private ownership system of the other.

An explorer whose voyage begins in Europe, and whose perspectives have been conditioned by the laws and customs of European nations, arrives in the New World and plants the flag of the European nation he represents. Is his claim of ownership for his home country legitimate? Residents of the home country may think so, but residents of the discovered country may not. How far does his claim of ownership for his homeland extend? Is the land he claims not already owned by natives of the New World? If indigenous peoples are present, have they already, in terms used by their own cultures, claimed ownership? If so, how far does their claim extend, and how many people must already live in the region to make it a viable claim? Is an ownership claim made by a single indigenous person living, say, 500 miles away, legitimate? Does a claim of ownership coming from a society in which the concept of ownership is vague and nonoperational take precedence over a competing claim whose origin is from a nation in which ownership is well defined and operational? Answer these questions one way and the explorer and his homeland have a legitimate claim of ownership of presently "unowned land"; answer them another way and they do not.

Even a culture that has long functioned on the basis of private ownership has conceptual and definitional problems with ownership. Can land once owned become unowned? Suppose the ownership claim to a parcel of vacant land has not been acted upon or asserted for decades. Does it revert to an unowned status, subject to claim by someone whose family has not before owned this land?

Migrants to the New World from Europe used land in the West to graze the cattle they had brought with them. They treated the land as open range land, which meant that cattle were allowed to graze in any stretch of land not already occupied by someone else's cattle. This imposed no problem, since the available land was plentiful relative to the demands put on it by grazing cattle. Farmers came to this land and sought to raise crops without having these crops destroyed by free-ranging cattle. They fenced in and staked claims to what had been unowned land. Are their claims of ownership valid? Should they have purchased the land from ranchers? Which ranchers? Oh, well, let them fight it out! And this is what they did until law began to take hold in this wilderness.[1]

Ownership is complex, and I do not have the knowledge required to answer the questions I have just put before the reader. A private ownership system is not delivered to a society in a finished, complete condition. It takes time, effort, and experience to develop a legal system that gives meaning to ownership and that is prepared to cope with ownership problems that are novel. Ownership and the legal system that underpins it are not to be taken for granted.

III

Ownership problems on which I can shed some light are usefully put into two categories: those that relate to the content of a privately owned bundle of rights and those that relate to the identity of the owner of the bundle. (In a way that is discussed below, one that is not generally appreciated by legal scholars, there is a logical and empirical relationship between content and owner identity.) Content refers to the bundle of rights a person has in the resource to which this bundle applies. Can the owner exclude all others from the use of this resource? Can the owner set any price for others to pay if they desire to use the resource? Can the owner build on a parcel of land and also mine it? Can he sell the right to build but retain the right to mine? Answers to questions such as these describe the content of the bundle of rights that someone owns. If we take the content of an ownership entitlement as a known given, there remains the problem of who owns the entitlement. Identity of owner refers to the specific person or persons who own the entitlement. John or Mary? Shareholders or corporate board members? Person or city government?

[1] The Western movie matinees I attended as a youth in Chicago always favored the farmers over the cattlemen.

I discuss content first. In a purely private ownership arrangement, the content of an owned bundle of rights includes exclusivity; exclusivity means that the owner of the resource may use it as he or she pleases (subject to whatever legal restrictions society may place on its use) and that those who do not own the resource cannot use it unless its owner has given them permission to use it. Ownership also includes alienability (again, subject to whatever legal restrictions society may place on alienability). Alienability is the right of the owner to offer his entitlement to the resource, or parts of this entitlement, to others.

A truncated bundle of ownership rights would be one in which an owner has the right to offer his or her entitlement for sale to others subject to a legal restriction that prevents the asking of a price in excess of some stipulated amount. A legal rent ceiling prevents the owner of an apartment building from offering his apartments for use by others at a rent that exceeds the stipulated ceiling price. A condition in which a person has the right to use a resource but not the right to bar others from using the resource also depicts a truncated bundle of ownership rights. A person may own a parcel of land but, by law, may be unable to prevent passage across the land by others.

These examples depict variation in the content of an entitlement and depict the difference between contents that are completely and only partially private. Social restrictions of one sort or another always impose restrictions on what an owner may do with a resource; so, as a practical matter, all ownership is comprised of a truncated bundle of rights. The complete bundle of private rights is nonetheless useful for deducing the consequences that flow from whatever restrictions society may place on the owner of a resource. The use made of a highway whose owner is entitled to bar drivers may be contrasted to the use made of the same highway from which drivers cannot be barred: a tollway versus a freeway. The private owner of a tollway, by asking users to pay a price for access, keeps the roadway less congested than does the public owner of a freeway who invites free access.[2]

There are many ways to truncate the bundle of ownership rights. Prominent among them is price control. This restricts the price at which the owner can offer the resources for sale or for use to others. A maximum legal price that is lower than the price that would arise in an unregulated market results in a demand for the resource, or for its use, that exceeds the amount of resource being offered for sale or for use. A queue forms of persons who desire to purchase the good or to use it at the legal price, but who cannot acquire it. An effective ceiling on the rent that apartment owners can ask potential renters, for example, creates a waiting "line" of apartment seekers.

The methods used by apartment owners to select persons in this queue surely will emphasize the income of potential renters less and other characteristics more than would be true if rents were allowed to rise to levels that would eliminate the queue. Landlords would find their interests better served by giving more attention to the number of children in the family seeking to secure living space, since children tend to damage apartments more than do childless older couples. Young adults who enjoy partying would be put toward the end of the queue along with large families. Apartment owners who have personal preferences for people of some colors and not others, of some religions and not others, and of some nationalities and not others are encouraged by effective rent ceilings to give greater weight to these considerations.

---

[2] Elsewhere I have called the truncated ownership that allows free use to all a "communal right" (Demsetz, 1967); Hardin (1968) describes the resource to which such a right attaches "a commons." However, he mistakenly uses the commons to critique Adam Smith's claim that independently acting, self-interested individuals in competitive pursuit of self-interest are led as if by an "invisible hand" to promote the public interest. Smith's "invisible hand" serves the public interest because he discusses it in the context of private ownership of resources. It is correct to deny this by referring to a situation in which private rights are truncated.

Personal characteristics of applicants become more important precisely because the law prevents them from compensating apartment owners for accepting persons with personal characteristics that are not favored.

Similarly, zero-priced access to freeways emphasizes nonprice methods of allocating scarce space. People will leave work earlier in order to occupy a space on the freeway before others attempt to enter the freeway, or they will leave work later to avoid the commuter congestion time of the day, or they will alter the location of where they live; all of these tactics result from a price (in this case a zero price) that is below the price that would bring the demand to use the roadway into equality with the use of the roadway at a level of traffic density that maximizes the value to drivers of having the roadway available.

While the above discussion emphasizes those consequences that flow from the truncating of ownership rights that many readers will not like, there are others that they may like. An owner of fuel may not use it to burn down a rival's factory. The owner of the factory may not offer to employ laborers who are below a young age. The owner of an automobile may not use it in a way that exceeds speed limits. All these restrictions truncate the bundle of ownership rights and, in doing so, have consequences. The reader may applaud some consequences and detest others.

Restrictions on content of ownership entitlements may change the type of people who choose to become owners, a consequence of restrictions that is not yet widely recognized. This interaction between content and owner identity occurs because restrictions usually alter the mix of rewards that owners can expect from the assets they own. Rent control, for example, reduces the cash reward relative to rewards that depend on the personal characteristics of renters. This implies that people who have no interest in the personal characteristics of renters will put a lower value on owning apartments in the presence of a rent ceiling than in the absence of the ceiling. People who have strong preferences for and against some personal characteristics will also put a lower value on owning apartments, but they will not reduce this value by as much as people who do not have strong preferences will. Put differently, rent controls make people interested in personal characteristics more willing to own apartment buildings than people who are not interested in personal characteristics, since some of the compensation received by the former – that which takes the form of the personal characteristics of those with whom one deals – is not subject to an analogous ceiling. People who have strong preferences for people of particular color, religion, age, and so on, or who have no qualms about breaking the law by receiving cash "under the table" from renters, will, in larger numbers, become owners of apartment buildings. While it is recognized that apartment owners will give more attention to personal characteristics of potential renters in a regime of rent control, it is not yet recognized that this effect is intensified by the fact that those who come to own apartments will tend to be those for whom personal characteristics make a difference.

Quite a long time ago, I began a study of apartment-for-rent advertising in the Chicago area, using the *Chicago Tribune* as my source of information. The study remains in my file, still uncompleted. It nonetheless is of interest to the topic of this essay. The period of time encompasses the World War II years. Common use was made during this time, and before it, of words such as "restricted." These made it clear that African Americans and Jews need not apply to rent an apartment. It was also a common practice for the landlord to offer furnished apartments and to specify the payments required for the use of the furniture. Just prior to World War II, the fraction of ads that used such words or that required purchase or rental of furniture was about 10 percent. With the introduction of rent controls during World War II, this fraction began to increase. Toward the end of the war, when servicemen and women began to return home and when, therefore, rent controls caused a much wider gap between quantity of rental apartments demanded and quantity available, the fraction of ads of this kind began to rise. Shortly after the end of World War II, the fraction rose to 90 percent. These data reveal the greater emphasis put on personal characteristics by rent control. They also may reveal a change in the type of people who own apartment buildings.[3]

Changing the content of ownership bundles can affect the uses made of resources in these ways, but this may not be true if the identity of owners is changed without there being a change in the content of entitlements. This issue brings the second category of problems discussed in this essay to the fore, those associated with owner identity. And this means I now turn to the writings of R. H. Coase.

IV

What difference, if any, does identity of owner make? R. H. Coase, in his important article "The Problem of Social Cost" (1960), brought this question to the attention of economists when he explained why the profession had mischaracterized the problem of externalities. His explanation deals with this problem under two alternative conditions, one in which the cost of using the price system is assumed to be zero and the other in which this cost is assumed to be positive. The positive cost case, with which I have some disagreement, is discussed in essay 7. In the zero cost case, I fully agree with Coase. My intent in discussing the zero cost case is to prepare the reader who has not yet become familiar with Coase's work to understand the more complex case in which the cost of using the price system is positive.

The problem discussed by Coase is exemplified by his discussion of *Sturges v. Bridgman*, decided by an English court in 1879. A

---

[3] A more serious examination of this phenomenon than the one I pursued would need to recognize other possible causes of these statistics, such as the large migration into Chicago of rural families from the South.

doctor had taken occupancy of a premise located next to one in which a confectioner conducted his business. Eight years after moving in, the doctor added a consulting and treating room to the original structure. This brought his work with patients into closer proximity to the confectioner's machinery. As a result, the noise coming from the confectioner's quarters interfered with the doctor's ability to diagnose illnesses of the chest and, the doctor claimed, made it difficult from him to think clearly about the medical problems brought to him by his patients. The court decided for the doctor, entitling him to more quiet than was allowed by the confectioner's equipment.

Coase then inquires as to the resource-use consequence of a court's decision in such cases, doing so by carefully thinking through a comparison of the consequences that would flow if the court favored one of the petitioners with the consequences that would flow if, instead, the court favored the second petitioner. The decision choice is not to be thought of as taking place sequentially through time but as a comparison of substitute decisions. Will resources be used in different ways depending on which of the two is favored? The intuitive answer to this question is "yes," and so was the answer implied by the externality doctrine that prevailed at the time Coase wrote. Coase's subtle reasoning shows this intuition to be wrong if the price system can be used as freely as neoclassical price theory assumes.

Both alternatives are consistent with a private property system. The process is not one of regulation, as neither decision insists on a court-defined *specific* decibel-level outcome. Given the court's decision, the parties can negotiate with each other to achieve some mutually acceptable decibel level. Who pays and who receives payment to achieve this level is determined by which alternative assignment of ownership rights the court has chosen. If the doctor is favored by the decision, the confectioner will need to pay the doctor if he wishes to make use of a noisy candy-making machine. Had the confectioner been favored by the court, the doctor would need to pay the confectioner to obtain a lowering of the decibel level. Hence, the court's decision has an effect on which way wealth flows between the two parties. The wealth distribution issue, however, is a diversion from the question Coase sought to answer; this was the effect of the court's decision on resource allocation. In this particular case, does the court's decision have an effect on the machinery used by the confectioner?

It was Coase's insight to see that freely entered negotiations between the parties would yield the same allocation of resources no matter which of the two possible decisions is chosen by the court. If the court favors the doctor, as it in fact did, the confectioner could nonetheless obtain permission from the doctor to continue using noisy candy-making machinery, and he would be able to secure this permission if the value he attaches to the use of noisy machinery exceeds the cost this noise imposes on the doctor. Given that this is the case, a mutually agreeable bargain can be struck that allows for a noisy environment. However, this would also be true if the court had favored the confectioner. In this case, the doctor would need to pay the confectioner to reduce the noise level. If we keep the measures of costs and benefits just used, we know the doctor would not be willing to pay enough to the confectioner to achieve this result because the noisy environment is less costly to the doctor than is the cost borne by the confectioner if the noisy candy-making machinery is not used. Either ruling the court can make will result in continued use of the noisy candy-making machine. The values assumed in these calculations can be changed so that a quiet environment results, but then the new values would result in a quiet environment no matter which of the alternative rulings the court chooses. Although the distribution of wealth is affected by the court's decision, the allocation of resources is not.

In retrospect this is all very clear. The private ownership system allocates resources to their highest value uses. And this use is the same no matter who owns the resources if ownership assignment has no significant wealth effects on the demands for medical services and candy.

The difference between this method of resolving conflicts and the approach customarily taken if regulation is used to influence the use of machinery may be noted. Regulation involves a law that makes noise levels above a certain amount illegal or that bars the use of noisy candy-making machines. It is illegal under this approach for the parties to the conflict to negotiate a solution that would yield high noise or that would allow for noisy machinery. Regulation also has an effect on wealth distribution, since the confectioner must forgo the use of cheap noisy candy-making machinery in favor of more expensive quiet machinery or the doctor must forgo building an extension that brings his office closer than "x" feet to the candy maker's place of business; here, the doctor, who would presumably need to build a second story at greater cost if he is to gain space, suffers a potential loss of wealth. Regulation has wealth consequences, but more than this, and unlike the common-law solution to a conflict over resource use, it also has resource allocation consequences. One regulation yields an outward extension of the doctor's premises coupled to quiet candy-making equipment, while the other regulation results in upward expansion of the doctor's premises coupled to noisy candy-making equipment. Resource allocation and wealth distribution both result from the regulatory approach.

The regulatory approach might by chance result in an efficient allocation of resources, but the common-law court approach certainly will if there is no cost to negotiating an agreement between contending parties. The level of noise that obtains after such negotiations is that which results in the highest possible joint value of the two activities; noisy equipment is abandoned only if its value to the confectioner is less than the value of quiet to the doctor, and noisy equipment is retained only if its value to the confectioner exceeds the value of quiet to the doctor. And, in terms of wealth distribution, the resource allocation that results from the court's decision holds whichever party is favored by the court.

The view of economists before Coase wrote on this topic was that the noise emanating from the confectioner's machinery imposed a cost on the neighboring doctor but not one that would be taken account of by the confectioner when choosing which machinery to use to make candy. The total social cost in this "two-person mini-world" consisted of the cost to the confectioner of purchasing and operating the candy-making machine and the cost to the doctor of noise emanating from the confectioner's machine.[4] On the then-accepted view of this type of problem, it would not be total social cost that influences the candy maker's equipment-purchasing decision but only the cost to him of making the purchase and buying the electricity used to power it. Since these costs take no account of the harm caused by the neighboring doctor, they are only part of the total cost borne by society from the use of noisy candy-making machinery. As a result, the confectioner would be inclined to purchase a noisy machine even if this resulted in an increase in total social cost. The cost borne by the doctor, which would in fact influence the confectioner's decision through negotiations between the two, was ignored by the then-existing doctrine of externalities. It was treated as external to the decision-making process, and this doctrine made the presumed difference between total social cost and total private cost the test of the presence of an externality problem.

Coase saw that if the court had decided in favor of the confectioner, it would have created an incentive for the neighboring doctor to offer a payment to the confectioner to lower the noise level (or to purchase a more expensive, quieter machine), such payment, in the limit, being equal to the cost borne by the doctor as

---

[4] The cost incurred by the doctor to extend the structure of his office becomes relevant if the analysis is forward-looking from the time the doctor merely considers whether to add a room. Implicitly taken by Coase is a cost incurred before the case arrives in court.

a result of the noise. Since the confectioner would not receive this payment should he invest in and use noisy machinery, he would in fact bear a cost for doing so that reflects damages done to the doctor. This is brought into the confectioner's profit calculations in the form of forgone revenue or as an implicit cost of using noisy machinery, and in this way it influences his decision about what type of machinery to use.

The discussion just concluded reveals a very important tendency of capitalism. On the assumption that people are in a better position to seek their interests than are people whom they have not employed to assist them, capitalism, by privatizing ownership of resources and allowing people to negotiate the uses to which these resources will be put, tends to guide resources into those uses that yield maximum marketplace values. I describe this conclusion as a strong tendency because we have not yet brought competition and monopoly into the discussion; the presence of monopoly can undermine this tendency.

The problem just discussed should be viewed from a forward-looking perspective in the sense that the locations of doctor and candy maker, and the equipment the candy maker will use, are yet to be determined. In this context it must be recognized that land owners, doctors, and candy makers will compete in the rental market or in the property-for-sale market. Since no doctor and no candy maker are yet neighbors, the locations they choose and the contracts they will write will be determined under competitive conditions. Supposing here that the cost of transacting is zero, we may conclude that competition between private owners of resources will yield an allocation of resources that maximizes the market value derived from these resources.

7 REINTERPRETING THE EXTERNALITY PROBLEM

C OASE'S REASONING, DISCUSSED IN ESSAY 6, REACHES THE
conclusion that resource allocation is unaffected by the identity of the person who is assigned the right to control the use of a
scarce resource if people can use markets and negotiations freely.
Furthermore, he concluded that there can be no difference between
social and private cost in such a world. It is a world without ineffi-
ciencies (and, by implication, without externalities). However, he
reaches a different conclusion for a world if the cost of using the
price system is positive. Inefficiency cannot be ruled out in this
more realistic world. This contrasting conclusion is now solidly
incorporated in economic doctrine. The present essay's objective is
to change doctrine in this respect.

Preliminary to doing this, some attention to terminology is
needed. In a work of mine, "The Cost of Transacting on the New
York Stock Exchange" (Demsetz, 1968), I empirically examined
the cost of using the NYSE to execute orders to buy and sell equity
shares. I called this cost "transaction cost," which seemed quite
natural for a market in which trading is so active. As my article
explained, I meant this to represent the cost of using the price system in the particular case of the NYSE. I continue to use transaction
cost to mean the cost of using the price system. Coase means by
this cost the value of resources used to obtain information about
prices and to engage in exchange at these prices. Coase describes

the cost of using the price system in his 1937 article on the firm. He writes:

The main reason why it is profitable to establish a firm would seem to be that there is a cost of using the price mechanism. The most obvious cost . . . is that of discovering what the relevant prices are . . . The costs of negotiating and concluding a separate contract for each exchange transaction which takes place on a market must also be taken into account.

And in his 1960 article about externalities he gives a similar notion:

In order to carry out a market transaction it is necessary to discover who it is that one wishes to deal with, to inform people that one wishes to deal with and to what terms, to conduct negotiations leading up to a bargain, to draw up the contract and undertake the inspection needed to make sure that the terms of the contract are being observed, and so on.

I use transaction cost to mean no more and no less than what Coase describes as the cost of using the price system. The stipulation is necessary because later writers broadened the meaning of transaction to include the costs of information and of cooperating between parties whether these costs are incurred in exchange across markets or in any other setting, such as in managing workers within a firm. Coase clearly meant to distinguish costs incurred to manage resources within the firm from costs incurred to interact across markets at market-determined prices, and I wish to preserve this distinction.

I

The main source of concern among economists about externalities is found in the writings of A. C. Pigou, especially in his *Economics of Welfare* (1920). Pigou viewed his work as a criticism of conclusions held by mainline economists of his day about the ability of a private-ownership, competitive economy to allocate resources efficiently. His central point was that the neoclassical model of this economic system is wrong in presuming that private decision makers take all costs and benefits into account when deciding how to use their resources. Because of this, we cannot conclude that resources will be allocated efficiently.

However, if an effect of using a resource is a cost or a benefit, there must be someone who experiences this effect. If so, this effect must be taken into account by someone, even if this is not the person who owns the resource whose use produces this effect. This means, if the cost of using the price system is zero, that there will emerge prices measuring each and every cost and/or benefit that arises in the course of interactions between persons. As discussed in essay 6, Coase showed that, in this case, all costs and benefits are taken into account when resources are allocated by way of a market-based price system. Efficient resource allocation results, or, as Coase puts it, the value derived from the use of resources is maximized. Coase also observed that if costs are incurred to use the price system, these effects, even though they are borne by someone, will not be entirely borne by the person whose use of resources gives rise to these effects.

A steel mill puts soot in the air in order to produce steel at the lowest possible cost, which, we may assume, requires the mill to use soft coal. The soot descends on neighboring laundries and increases the cost to them of laundering cloths. The owner of the steel mill takes the price of coal into account and will take the increased cost borne by launderers into account if the cost of using the price system is zero, for then a launderer will offer payments to the owner of the steel mill if he will reduce the amount of soft coal he uses, such payments being determined by the cost increases borne by a launderer as a result of soot. However, these payments might not be forthcoming in sufficient amounts to accomplish this if a launderer must incur a cost, call it a transaction cost, to negotiate with the owners of the steel mill. This suggests that markets may not bring all costs and benefits borne by some people to bear on those whose use of resources brings these into existence. Coase concludes because of this incomplete reckoning that resources may not be allocated efficiently.

Coase was critical of neoclassical theory for neglecting the cost of using the price system, but I think he is wrong about this. Neoclassical theory is written as if there is no cost of using the price system, but the theory could be rephrased to take account of transaction cost if it shared Coase's objective. Coase seeks to explain when a price system will be used and when it will not. Neoclassical theory seeks to explain the allocation of resources *if there is a price system that transmits to all the costs and benefits* that arise from the way in which resources are allocated. The two tasks differ. Even so, neoclassical theory could be turned to the task of understanding resource allocation if prices are available only at a cost. This is what I intend to do.

II

It is of course true that positive transaction cost will keep negotiations between interacting parties from being as finely tuned as they would be if transactions could be executed freely; indeed, if high enough, transaction cost may block negotiations completely. However, it is incorrect to infer from this that resources are allocated inefficiently. Missing from Coase's and from the contemporary treatment of this situation is a recognition that efficiency itself requires foregoing fine-tuning of the sort that would be appropriate (efficient) in a world in which transaction cost were zero. This point, made some time ago, has not penetrated discussions of externalities.

Transaction cost is no different from other costs in regard to determining which good or service is to be produced. If the cost of producing a hydrogen-fueled automobile exceeds the price that people are willing to pay for the vehicle, efficient resource allocation requires that this vehicle not be produced. Similarly, efficient resource allocation requires that a transaction not take place if the cost of producing the transaction exceeds the price that people are willing to pay to engage in exchange. We do not shout "inefficiency!" if the vehicle is not produced. Why proclaim inefficiency if a transaction is not produced?[1]

The source of confusion about this is the fact that Coase has embedded the externality problem in a hypothetical experiment involving alternative assignments of ownership rights. The counterexample pointed to in the preceding paragraph regarding a hydrogen-fueled automobile is not directed at the issues raised if we ask what difference it makes if X has the right to put a car on the street or if Y has this right. This issue, which involves who owns which rights, simply does not come to the surface when dealing with standard production problems. Coase embeds the externality problem in a model in which the assignment of rights is involved. Although this difference leads to somewhat different conclusions, these do not bear on the question of efficiency. This claim needs to be examined in a bit more detail.

Coase sees the possibility of inefficiency arising in a situation in which there are competing claimants for control of a scarce resource. They take their dispute to court, which assigns ownership rights to one of the claimants. In this case, however, Coase assumes that the cost for these parties to negotiate (i.e., transact) with each other after the court has made its decision is prohibitively high. Suppose the court assigns ownership to the party who is unable to put the involved resource to its highest value use. That is, the product this party produces with this resource is less valuable (in the marketplace) than is the product that would have been produced by the other party had he or she been favored by the court. One

---

[1] "For produced goods . . . optimality theorems require equalities among various marginal rates of substitution. . . . [but] do not . . . for goods and services that are not produced in the final efficient equilibrium; for these goods we have corner solutions involving inequalities . . . a premise of requiring equalities is that we are talking about goods which we require to be produced in positive quantities" (Demsetz 1964).

may wonder why either party is unable to put the resource to the same uses as the other party, but this objection is not in the spirit of Coase's discussion and we may set it aside.[2] Setting this aside, we can have no objection to Coase's conclusion that the resource may not be put to its highest value use. This is because high transaction cost prevents the party whom the court favored from selling the entitlement to the party whom the court did not favor but who can use the resource to create goods that are more valuable. If we stay with the framework in which he has cast this problem, we must agree with Coase that more value could have been secured from the resource if the court had made the opposite decision. The error is in identifying this as an inefficiency of the economic system that is brought about by the cost of transacting. Coase may be quoted on this (1960, p. 16):

In these conditions [of positive transaction cost] the initial delimitation of legal rights does have an effect on the efficiency with which the economic system operates. One arrangement of rights may bring about a greater value of production than any other. But unless this is the arrangement of rights established by the legal system, the costs of reaching the same result . . . through the market may be so great that [this arrangement of rights] may never be achieved.

I suspect that Coase may not have carefully reviewed the phraseology he uses to describe this conclusion, a rare event indeed. Nonetheless, his statement has brought economists to the conclusion that positive transaction cost can make the competitive economic system function inefficiently, since a lesser valued mix of goods is produced than would have been produced if transaction cost had not hampered the market's ability to reassign ownership rights. Coase puts his conclusion thus: "the initial delimitation of

---

[2] The required inability may derive from purely personal differences in the utility derived from the way a resource is used, but then the value derived from personalizing the rewards of using the resource one way instead of another should be taken into account when addressing the efficiency question.

legal rights does have an effect on the efficiency with which the economic system operates." The profession has accepted this phrasing and, based on it, the prevailing doctrine is that positive transaction cost can undermine the efficiency of the economic system.

But wait! With each alternative assignment of ownership, the economic system does the best that can possibly be done. The private-ownership, competitive economic system does allocate resources efficiently *given the court's decision*. If the court has errantly chosen ownership, well then, the economic system at least minimizes the loss borne by society because of the court's error. Under the stated conditions, this loss is minimized by forgoing market transactions whose purpose would be to reshuffle ownership entitlements, since, by assumption, the cost of reshuffling more than exhausts the increment in the value of goods that will result. *Legal error* has caused the problem, not positive transaction cost. There is no inefficiency in the way the market accommodates to the court's mistake.

How does the situation described by Coase differ from a government policy that affects the distribution of wealth? Special interest groups petition the state for a tax-and-spend policy that is expected to yield benefits. The state responds, and the mix of goods and the distribution of wealth that results will differ depending on just how the state responds. One response may make more valuable uses of resources than other responses. We do not conclude that the economic system is inefficient if it produces the most valuable mix of goods that is possible *given the response chosen by the government*. Coase's assignment of entitlements by the court constitutes a distribution-of-wealth decision and, because of the difference in the assumed production capabilities of the plaintiffs, it also influences the mix of goods that is produced if transaction cost is positive. No matter how the court decides and no matter if transaction cost is zero or positive, the competitive decentralized economy is efficient in that it makes the assigned distribution of wealth yield the most valuable mix of output that is possible given the cost of using the market to reverse the court's decision.

The legal system is the institution that resolves the conflict over ownership entitlement. However, neoclassical economic theory implicitly assumes the existence of well-defined ownership rights. Care must be taken not to confuse the two situations. Coase's 1937 discussion of the make-or-buy decision faced by the firm (discussed later) does not mix these two problems. He imaginatively reveals the way in which the cost of using the price system affects the internal structure of the firm. In this application, however, ownership entitlements are assigned and in place; there is no contesting of these in courts. And in that article, Coase does not at all speak of transaction cost as a source of inefficiency in the way a firm resolves the make-or-buy decision. In his article on externalities, however, he brings the court into the picture by posing an ownership entitlement problem. This allows the court to make a mistake.

The quality of the court's decision, however, has nothing to do with how well the market works to bring social and private costs into equality. The court is not part of the economic system. The legal system, after all, is designed to be publicly provided and to be insulated from the price system, just as is the government when it puts a wealth distribution policy into effect. We do not know what motivates a court other than some earlier court decision with which it hopes to be consistent. If the court were brought into the economic system, say by allowing contesting parties to bid for the court's decision, the court would not make the mistake that is essential to Coase's logic, since the party who can make the most valuable use of the entitlement will be able to offer more to the court. I do not necessarily recommend making the court part of the economic system, but consideration of this option fully reveals that the court in Coase's discussion is not part of the economic system. We cannot conclude from the consequences of an error made by the court that the economic system is responsible for the lower value mix of output that results.

Given that the court lies outside the economic system, what really is the "inefficiency" that Coase (mistakenly) attributes to the economic system? It is that the market does not tolerate the bearing of transaction cost to correct for the court's error if the cost of doing so exceeds the gain in the value that is to be expected from realigning the ownership of the entitlement. The market is accused of being inefficient because it is efficient!

III

Coase goes on to write:

It is clear that an alternative form of economic organisation which could achieve the same result at less cost than would be incurred by using the market [to realign ownership entitlements] would enable the value of production to be raised. As I explained many years ago, the firm represents such an alternative.... Another alternative ... is direct Government regulation. (1960, p. 16)

However, he should have rewritten:

It is clear that an organization alternative to the court such, perhaps, as the government or the firm, that could assign control of resources with less error, would enable the value of production to be raised.

He does not explain how this might be accomplished, nor does he note that the source of the problem *is* a nonmarket institution, namely, the court. It is unclear to me how the firm accomplishes the task. Once the court has made its decision, the party who has received the entitlement, if it is a firm, might merge with the party who has not received it, another firm, thus conveying control of the entitlement to the party who can put it to best use. However, this requires the equivalent of an exchange of assets, and so, it requires an encounter with the same high level of transaction cost that barred a market-based exchange. Alternatively, the contesting parties, prior to going to court, might settle their dispute by merging, or by exchanging, assets. However, this again incurs market transaction cost. The only advantage I see for this method as compared to a market-based purchase and sale is that it avoids a trip to the court.

Coase must have had an entirely different role for the firm in mind. The firm's owner listens to two middle managers' plea for control of some of the firm's resources. The owner chooses one pleader over the other. The favored pleader then uses the resources he or she has been assigned and produces an output that has some market value. If this market value is judged by the owner to be greater than it would have been if the other pleader had been favored, all is well and good. If it is judged to be less than expected, the owner reassigns control to the pleader who, before, had been disfavored. Resources therefore end up generating the highest possible value. How does this differ from a situation in which the court has assigned an entitlement and then is asked, at some future time, to reconsider the case? The difference is in the fact that the firm's activities are part of the economic system in as much as the firm's owner is interested in maximizing the market value of the goods the firm makes, while the court is organized in ways that discourage the plaintiffs from bidding for the court's decision. The difference does not lie in transaction cost, since the owner of the firm incurs the equivalent of transaction cost when reconsidering a prior decision and acting to remedy it; if this reconsideration cost is too high, the owner, like the court, will not reconsider. In which case, if we followed the terminology adopted by Coase when discussing the court, we would (mistakenly) claim that the firm (or is it the market?) is inefficient.

The only true alternative to the marketplace is an institution that can use a greater measure of *coercion* than is available to participants in the marketplace. This, in fact, may be a firm, but it surely is the state. The court's error might be expeditiously rectified by the government through coercive means that, depending on how one measures the cost of using these means, might be less costly than using voluntarily struck agreements. Yet, the foundation of a private-ownership, market-based economy is its generally superior ability to work with resources as compared with central planners, and that it can do a better job while preserving a greater measure of freedom for individuals. I write "generally" because the state has a role to play. This will not generally be in activities the equivalent of producing food or steel unless the use of slave labor does reduce the real cost (including that part borne by the slaves) of production, and even in this case the state would be unneeded since workers would then agree voluntarily to work under slavelike conditions. Anyway, this possibility has nothing to do with externalities. The state might be able to organize transactions more cheaply than can markets, but I see no reason for this to be the case.

The case for the state is strongest in the presence of high costs of barring free riders, costs I would describe as high ownership costs, not as high transaction costs, since the two types of costs need not correlate strongly.[3] Soot from a steel mill descends on a neighboring laundry and raises the cost of laundering. There is a transaction cost that must be borne if this cost is to play a role in decisions made by the owner of the steel mill (if the mill is entitled to use soft coal when producing steel), but there is no free-rider problem. The demand for soot reduction will become evident in the negotiations between the two parties if the transaction cost is reasonably low, and there is no reason to think that the state can bring the parties together at less cost than can the market. Now, suppose that multiple laundries surround the steel mill. Each laundry owner has a strategic interest in underrevealing what he or she is willing to pay to have soot reduced, hoping that other laundry owners will purchase a desired amount of reduction in soot. A psychological preference for behaving strategically cannot

[3] See Demsetz (1964).

reasonably be interpreted as a cost of using the price system as Coase describes this cost. If it is anything more than a psychological propensity, then it is a cost of having multiple laundries in the vicinity of a steel mill. In this case, the state can force a solution that is better than the market's if we make the heroic assumptions that the state knows what it is doing and seeks an efficient mix of steel output and laundry services. The state applies an appropriate tax to the use of coal in the manufacture of steel, as Pigou suggested.

This is not just a definitional issue, one in which strategic behavior, if one chooses, can be called a cost of using the price system. Strategic behavior is entirely different from the cost of soliciting price information and concluding an exchange; it is a problem of strategic provision of misleading price information. But if the reader insists on confusing the two, so be it, but, then, please remember that situations in which strategic behavior is important are but a part, and a small part at that, of all situations that involve positive transaction cost.

8 FIRMS AND HOUSEHOLDS AS SUBSTITUTES

L ITTLE ATTENTION WAS GIVEN TO FIRMS AND HOUSEHOLDS by economists until the middle part of the twentieth century, even though these institutions have a role to play in the theory of the economic system that emerged toward the end of the discipline's neoclassical period. The firm was not completely neglected, but discussions of it did not mature to the point at which the existence of the firm and its inner organization became important enough to integrate the firm into the theory of the economic system except in a very limited way. My purpose in this essay, however, is not to trace the rise of the firm as a topic of interest to economists but, rather, to discuss the current role of transaction cost in explaining the existence and organization of firms.

I

The first serious attempt to explain the firm's existence and organization was offered by F. H. Knight in his work *Risk, Uncertainty, and Profit* (1921), but this emerges as a byproduct of Knight's inquiry into the true source of profit (and loss). Contrary to then-popular views, which identified profit as the reward for risk taking, Knight identified uncertainty as the source. Uncertainty, to Knight, differs from risk. It is the outcome of conditions about which so little is known that there are no data on which to base probabilistic calculations that allow one to calculate risks of the sort against which firms offer insurance. Risk taking cannot explain profit, according to Knight, because probabilistic predictions of risks transform the cost of risk into just another cost of doing business, a cost that will often appear in the form of insurance premiums. Competition between firms will lead, in equilibrium, to revenues that are just sufficient to cover the costs, including in these the insurance-type premiums paid to shift risks to someone or some company holding a diversified portfolio of risk obligations. Hence, the presence of risk in a competitive setting offers no source of true profit. Uncertainty, to Knight, is necessary to the existence of both profit and/or loss because the occurrence and impact of events that are not statistically predictable cannot be insured against. Profit arises if uncertainty reveals itself in events that unpredictably increase revenues or reduce costs. Loss arises if these events unexpectedly reduce revenues or increase costs. If profits and losses are completely unpredictable, they cannot be eliminated by competitive entry and exit from markets.

Hypothetically, in Knight's explanation, profit, viewed as a general outcome of business uncertainty, reflects a psychological disposition among businesspeople to take a pessimistic view of the future. This leads them to underinvest, as judged by the unpredictable opportunities that in fact emerge. Underinvestment yields future prices that exceed future costs, and, thereby, profit. The existence of loss, in contrast, reflects a psychological disposition among businesspeople to take an overly optimistic view, leading future costs to exceed future prices. Psychology controls outcomes because statistically scientific predictions cannot be marshaled to temper optimism and pessimism. The equilibrium outcome is a general level of profit that is zero, which can obtain only if investors are unbiased in their guesses about the future. Although Knight does not explicitly offer a rationale for firms to exist, his argument implies their existence if they are suitable institutions through which optimistic gamblers can bet on the unknown future. The more optimistic they are, or the greater the number of optimists among them, the larger will be the number of firms and the greater will be the likelihood that the general level of correctly calculated profit is negative. Knight, in fact, states that he believes that true profit, calculated correctly over long stretches of time, is negative, but he makes no attempt to verify this.

Internal organization is an aspect of firms that should be distinguished from the question of whether an institution is a firm because a set of institutions may qualify as firms but rely on different internal organizations. Basic characteristics of the organization of firms are explained by Knight in terms of the *differences* that exist across people in their attitudes toward risk and uncertainty. The optimistic gamblers are more willing to bear risk and uncertainty. Possibly because of their psychologies, or possibly because of their wealth, they have a comparative advantage in risk bearing. They do so by becoming the investors-owners-managers of firms, ready to claim profit or to bear loss should either occur. Those less inclined to gamble become employees; they receive wage compensation that is largely, if not entirely, insulated from swings between profit and loss. Investors-owners-managers obtain the services of employees at lower wage costs than if employees shared fully in the ups and downs of profit; the investors-owners-managers of firms provide workers with a sort of firm-sponsored insurance against wide fluctuations in wages, and so, employees are willing to work for a smaller explicit wage. In return for this stability "guarantee," owners-managers insist that they should be able to direct and monitor the efforts of workers. This organizational arrangement accords with what is common practice in the business world. On Knight's explanation, the practice allows for the efficient distribution of risk and uncertainty among risk bearers.

II

Although Knight's *Risk, Uncertainty, and Profit* was much discussed by economists and others when it appeared, the discussion dealt mainly with risk and uncertainty and not with firms. Another decade was to pass before the inner organization of firms became an important topic in economics. This occurred when Berle and Means, in 1932, published their influential book *The Modern Corporation and Private Property*, a work that dealt with problems quite different from those that interested Knight. The division of control between shareholders and management in the modern corporation was the book's central topic. In fact, Knight did briefly discuss and dismiss this problem by noting that owners of firms get the managers they want; these managers may be lazy or careless, but their presence in the firm is not independent of, but is a result of, the exercise of control by owners. Any degree of freedom that is built into manager contracts is there because it suits the owners, and so there is no real separation between ownership and control. (This topic comes to the fore in the essay on the corporation.)

The Berle and Means book did not attempt to contribute to the theory of the firm. It noted that the modern corporation seems quite different from the firm as it appears in neoclassical economic theory; in neoclassical theory the firm always succeeds in maximizing profit by following the guidance provided by market-determined input and output prices. It was R. H. Coase, in his article "The Nature of the Firm," which appeared in 1937, five years after the Berle and Means book, who broached the twin topics of the existence and organization of the firm.

Coase's article begins with a critique of neoclassical theory for its failure to explain why firms should exist in an economy that neoclassical theory depicts as organized solely by way of reliance on the price system. His interpretation of neoclassical theory is that owners of resources are guided by market prices to use their resources in the most efficacious and efficient ways. On his view, people interact indirectly through the ways in which they react to market-given prices. No conscious management of some by others is needed. Looked at thusly, the firm is an institution in which some manage the activities of others; management of some by others seems to find no justification in neoclassical theory. I will return to critically assess this definition of the firm, but I note here that it excludes firms owned by a single person who, by him- or herself, does all the work required to turn out goods. If I were to ask the reader of this essay whether Cambridge University Press, its publisher, is a firm, I am confident that his or her answer would not be, "Well, after all, doesn't Cambridge Press employ many people?" More likely, the reply would be, "Well, after all, did Cambridge Press not publish this book and offer it for sale?" The distinction here is between defining a firm by its insider organization and defining it by its function in society.

The dictates of the price system are so compelling in neoclassical theory that one may wonder that the theory even refers to firms, so there is justification in Coase's complaints about neoclassical theory. However, the problem with neoclassical theory is not its failure to provide a reason for firms to exist but its failure to make explicit the reason it does offer. Coase is quite explicit about the reason he offers. The existence and importance of firms in the economic system, he explains, is due to the fact that the price system is not free. My intent in this essay is to highlight the theory of the firm that is implicit in neoclassical theory and to show that incorrect deductions have been drawn about firms by those who rely on the cost of using the price system to explain the existence of the firm.

III

Economist-readers who have been around as long as I have will remember, if they still can, the starting point of texts from which many of us learned principles of economics. These began with a circular flow diagram in which firms sell goods to households (in return for money payments from households) and in which households supply inputs, such as investment funds and labor services, to firms (in return for payments from firms). Markets and prices provide the interfaces that facilitate these flows. The diagram's purpose was to emphasize the role of markets and prices. Little note was taken of another aspect of it. This is its implicit treatment of firms as institutions that exist to specialize in the production of goods that are destined for use by households. Specialization here means the production of large numbers of units of a good most or all of which will be used by people who have no hand in its production.

This provides a rationale for the existence of firms that is quite different from that which Knight, Coase, and others offer. Firms exist in neoclassical theory *because specialization is productive.* If specialization were not productive, goods would be produced more cheaply in quantities small enough to be used exclusively by those who produce them; that is, households would be self-sufficient. A world consisting of self-sufficient households does not comprise an economic *system.* It especially does not constitute an economic system that reflects the problem that attracted the interest and efforts of economists: that of understanding how a price system coordinates the uses made of scarce resources by persons who, while not controlling others, are nonetheless dependent on the aggregation of the decisions that others make. This dependency arises because of the productivity of specialization. Neoclassical theory constructed a model of the firm that would serve as a tool in explaining both the manner in which interactions occur between interacting independent producers and households and the nature of the outcomes that resulted from these interactions. Consequently, it focused on interaction between decision-making entities and not on the organization within these entities. This is why it showed little interest in what goes on inside firms. Why a firm is organized in this way or that way simply is not a question that neoclassical theory entertains. The theory merely assumes that, however a firm is organized, it correctly responds to the price signals it receives from input and output markets. It treats the internal operations of the firm as if they constituted an accurate calculating machine because its interest is in the price system, not in the firm. The theory may be criticized for not dealing with a question as important as one that asks how the firm actually produces a good, but not for failing to contain within it a meaningful definition of firms and an implicit explanation of why they exist. In particular, the theory is not concerned with whether firms are single person institutions or manyperson institutions, and if it were pushed to examine this issue it probably would appeal to a combination of scale economies, transaction cost, and team productivity.

It should be clear from neoclassical theory's implicit "specialization is productive" explanation of the existence of firms that firms can exist only if the cost of using the price system (or transaction cost) is not prohibitively high. Indeed, *zero transaction cost* would make it possible to realize all firm-specific advantages of specialization by enabling firms to reach more households with the goods they produce. Zero transaction cost maximizes the importance of firms in the economic system by raising the percentage of total output of goods produced within specialized production units as compared to the percentage produced within self-sufficient households.

This is completely contrary to conclusions that economists have drawn from Coase's work; they see a zero cost of transacting as a reason for not employing workers and, therefore, for not relying on management of some by others. This, in turn, leads them to conclude that the price system substitutes for management in the production of goods. Markets are viewed as substitutes for firms; markets will be substituted for firms as the cost of using the price system declines. The substitution is thought of as reducing the importance of firms in the economy; in the extreme of zero transaction cost, firms are thought to be completely absent. The prime example of this perspective is the decrease in degree of vertical integration that is caused by a reduction in transaction cost. The vertically integrated firm produces its own inputs, combining these to produce the product that will be offered to potential buyers. This makes sense only if there is a cost to transacting across markets to acquire these inputs from other firms (that might specialize in making them). A reduction in transaction cost, therefore, leads to the substitution of markets for production within the firm.

It is a mistake, however, to interpret this as the equivalent of a reduction in the degree to which the economy relies on firms to produce the goods that people use. What it does imply is that fewer, more vertically integrated firms are substituted for more, less vertically integrated firms. It cannot be concluded from this that a reduction in the cost of transacting reduces the fraction of total output coming from firms. Indeed, a reduction in the cost of transacting has the opposite effect. It increases the output coming from firms relative to that coming from self-sufficient households. The reduction in transaction cost increases the number of less vertically integrated firms, but more goods produced by these firms reach more households because transaction cost is low.

By the same reasoning, an increase in the cost of transacting has effects opposite to those thought to follow from transaction cost economics. Fewer, more vertically integrated firms are substituted for more numerous, less vertically integrated firms, but the quantities of goods that are sold to households are reduced. Firms become less, not more, important in the economic system as the transaction cost increases. In the limit, an infinitely high cost of transacting will put all production in self-sufficient households, production and consumption becoming completely vertically integrated within each household. We may consider a particular example of this.

A legal (and effective) ceiling on apartment rents, because it limits the revenue the owners of apartment buildings can secure from ordinary tenants, encourages an owner to use the building as his own residence and/or as a residence for members of his family. This is an increase in the degree of vertical integration within the household, or, more generally, this is an increase in the degree of self-sufficiency. Firms, conceptualized as specialized owners of apartment buildings whose space is made available for rent to others, become less important in the economic system. In the general case, the greater is the difference between the regulated price and the market-clearing price, whether this difference is positive or negative, the greater is the increase in self-sufficiency throughout the economy. At the limit, as the difference between the two prices becomes larger, scale-favoring production techniques, of the sort that explain the existence of firms, are no longer worthwhile. Organizations specialized to owning apartment space for others to use become untenable (or untenanted). Firms become less important, and so do market prices, as sources of information. An economic system that relies completely on self-sufficient provision of living spaces emerges, and, because scale-favoring cost reductions are not used, poverty becomes more severe.

IV

One source of error in Coase's perspective is to see firms (or managements of firms) and prices (or the price system) as substitutes for each other in the task of allocating resources to production. They are not. Management uses prices as a source of information along with other sources. Prices are a source of information about opportunities, but, being simple conveyors of information, they are incapable of allocating resources; only people (in human activities) allocate resources. The true substitutes in the allocation of resources to the task of producing goods are (1) *people* who produce goods for others (i.e., in firms, whether or not more than one person does the producing) and (2) *people* who produce goods for themselves (i.e., in self-sufficient households).

A second source of error is to identify the firm and to assess its importance by degree of vertical integration or, what is the same thing, by degree of reliance on management of resources. This view implies that the complete absence of firms from an economic system can be imagined only if there is a complete absence of vertical integration. What could this possibly mean? Each and every task, no matter how small or brief, can be subdivided again and again. A positive degree of vertical integration is always with us because its absence requires the existence of an undividable "atom" of a task or activity. To identify a firm by the presence of vertical integration, then, implies that firms always exist.

No similar quandary is faced if a firm is identified as an institution that produces goods for sale to others; complete absence of firms on this view results from the absence of gains from specialization. This condition can be imagined; it implies, to repeat myself, that high transaction cost can only diminish the importance of firms even while it encourages vertical integration.

To these errors, a third should be added: identifying the firm as a manyperson organization. The error is easy to slip into because transaction cost economics (mistakenly) views the firm as the institution in which the management of some people by others displaces the "management" of people by the price system. And, of course, managers do manage people; hence, the firm is seen as a manyperson organization. This "of course" is, of course, incorrect. People manage inanimate resources as well as they do other people. It is a mistake to identify the presence of management in the production process as the management of some people by others. One person, without the help of employees, manages his or her resources. If these resources are put to the task of producing goods for sale to others, this person constitutes a firm as this is implicitly judged by neoclassical theory.

It is desirable to reaffirm here that transaction cost does play an important role in understanding the internal organization of firms, and that this role is correctly assessed by way of transaction cost analysis. By this I mean that transaction cost economics contributes to our understanding of the degrees to which firms are vertically integrated and to which they rely on the management of some by others. In regard to these issues, Coase's contribution is important, but it is not needed to explain the existence of firms, whose defining function is simply to produce goods for sale to others. Transaction cost does influence the importance of firms in the economic system, but the application of transaction cost analysis to the question of importance has led those who rely on transaction cost explanation to reach conclusions that are the opposite of those that are correct. Correct conclusions flow quite naturally if firms are defined by social function rather than by internal organization. And, finally, transaction cost analysis based on an internal organization definition of the firm offers no explanation for the existence of households or for the division of output between what is produced for one's self and what is produced for others.

v

An important issue remains untouched by this essay, the ownership of the firm. Neoclassical theory treats the firm as if it were a proprietorship, one in which the proprietor somehow allocates resources so as to minimize the cost of producing any specific rate of output and chooses the rate of output that maximizes the firm's profit, and, to a considerable extent, so does transaction cost theory. Transaction cost theory offers an explanation for why some firms are manyperson institutions in the sense of many workers being directed in their activities by "management." A question about the ownership structure of a firm like the public corporation is not contemplated by neoclassical theory or by transaction cost economics.

There is something in the label "public" that suggests a level of social responsibility above that of serving those willing to pay for the cost of producing goods. This view has been promoted in contemporary times by champions of a "stakeholder" view of the corporation. On this view, the corporation is responsible for pursing the interests not only of its shareholders, but also of others whose lives are affected by how the corporation uses its resources.

The proprietorship comes closest to the idealized firm of neo-classical and transaction cost theories; the partnership is somewhat different; and the corporation is very different. In the proprietorship, ownership and control are united in a single person, the firm's owner. This makes it plausible that the firm's resources are put to use in ways sought by the firm's owner. Partnerships, closed corporations, and public corporations use increasingly complex ownership arrangements, ownership being a shared responsibility to various degrees in them. An imperative of joint ownership is the development of a method for resolving differences in opinions among the several joint owners about what is to be done with the firm's resources. The public corporation involves so many shareholders that it is not usually practical to rely on consultations and discussions to resolve differences of opinion. Moreover, many of its shareowners do not desire to partake in business decisions and, in fact, do not do so often. The complexity of the public corporation's ownership structure gives rise to questions about who it is that really owns the corporation. This question and others are discussed in the essay on the corporation.

9 THE CONTRAST BETWEEN FIRMS
AND POLITICAL PARTIES

POLITICIANS AND POLITICAL PARTIES COMPETE, JUST AS DO firms. There is division of opinion about the consequences of this. Some think this gives voters the policies and management of these policies that they want, just as competition between firms is thought to deliver products they want at the lowest possible costs of producing them. Thus, Joseph Schumpeter (1950) writes:

[T]he social meaning or function of parliamentary activity is no doubt to turn out legislation and, in part, administrative measures. But in order to understand how democratic politics serve this social end, we must start from the competitive struggle for power and office and realize that the social function is fulfilled, as it were, incidentally – in the same sense that production is incidental to the making of profits.

Surely, Schumpeter oversimplifies. Private goods, in the main, are divisible. To the limits allowed by scale economies, their production can be tailored to individual wants. The output of the state, in the main, is indivisible; the public-good nature of policy and of its administration cannot be tailored to individual wants. Serving political majorities necessarily disappoints political minorities. Even the median voter model has winners and losers.

Stigler (1971) and other writers modify the analogy, contending that political policies respond to special interests, either because special interests deliver more votes or because they deliver more financial support. In this case, special interests get what they want.

The Contrast Between Firms and Political Parties

This is not necessarily what minorities or even majorities of voters want, but this view differs from the first only in terms of "currency." The first uses ballots, the second uses dollars and/or influence. Both views share a belief that politicians and parties are not independent principals in the political game. They are agents of other constituencies. Later work preserves this agency status but makes winning politicians and political parties the agents of a weighted combination of special interests and the general voting public. The view that abandons agency status is one that introduces information and voting costs, in the presence of which politicians have some freedom to serve their own interests; in this sense they become quasi principals.

In this essay I argue, on grounds different from information cost, that political parties exercise a degree of independence from voters, and that the degree is greater than that which business firms can exercise with respect to consumers. I base this argument on the difference in the ways political parties and business firms are organized.

I

There is little need to dwell on what I mean by a firm, although the boundary between what goes on within firms and what transpires across markets is unclear.[1] The firm in this essay is an institution that uses resources to produce and market goods in an attempt to profit its owners. This notion serves my purpose and is sufficiently accurate, but it rules out firms that have owners who derive personal utility from the specific goods the firm produces.

[1] A firm employs a person to take care of its grounds, directing him about how often to trim the shrubs, mow the grass, and fertilize each. The firm could have accomplished the same object by contracting with a grounds maintenance firm to provide the same services. The latter arrangement is thought of as organized by way of the price system; the former is thought of as organized by way of business management; but, unless the law distinguishes in some relevant way between an employment contract and a service contract, there really is not much difference between them.

A newspaper sometimes is owned and operated by a family whose objective, although welcoming of profit, is to foment change in the political attitudes of its readers. It does not seek to profit from giving readers what they want, although it certainly does accept profit. Instead, it seeks to change the social preferences of people, and this may require its family-owner to accept less profit than if it merely catered to the existing wants of readers.

Many firms do advertise their products, and in doing so they also seek to get potential purchasers to favor their products over those of other firms. However, they do so in the hope of profiting from the additional sales. The firms I seek to set aside engage in missionary work whose objective is not profit but a change in attitudes. The increase in utility realized by the newspaper's owners in this way could be converted into a monetary value that measures just how much profit they are willing to sacrifice to convert the social preferences of their readers, and, when this sum is added to the dollar profit made by selling newspapers, we could say that the newspaper's owners do seek to maximize profit. However, the substance of the distinction I make is that missionary zeal is very unimportant to what goes on in the vast majority of business firms, and so I will ignore it. This turns out to be useful because the behavior of a political party is influenced much more strongly by missionary zeal.

The political party is more difficult to define than is the firm. What I mean by a political party is a collection of people who co-operate to win political office *and* to shape the philosophical and sociological preferences of voters. This rules out those who, although they may vote for the party, make no commitment of time and effort to help the party's ongoing campaign, and those who, although they do give time and effort to the party, do so only for the wages they receive in return. "Outsiders" who reliably make financial contributions to a party or who provide it with continuing intellectual support are more qualified to be considered party members than are voters and wage-seeking secretaries and pollsters.

Three points of difference between firms and parties play a role in what is said below. Two have already been mentioned, the public-good aspect of political output and the missionary aspect of political parties. The missionary factor is important to political parties and unimportant to business firms. The public-good nature of output of political parties differs from the fundamentally private-good nature of output of business firms. You drive a Buick; I drive a Ford. You buy a home; I rent an apartment. The third point of difference is ownership. There is no owner of a political party in the sense of someone able to offer the party for sale to others or someone who bears most of the consequences of the party's success or failure.

II

We may begin discussing the consequences of these differentiating factors by distinguishing between the internal and external constituencies of firms and parties. Potential purchasers of goods (produced by firms) and potential consumers of programs (produced by parties) are the external constituencies. The internal constituencies are employees, owners of firms, and members of political parties.

Potential purchasers of goods have a powerful role in determining what goods firms produce, whereas employees of firms have only a minor role. Firms that do not produce what potential buyers want, or that do not sell what these buyers want at prices that are competitive with other firms, lose market share. If they persist in offering people that which they do not want, the firms fail to receive revenues that cover costs and they go out of business. This is so even if some of a firm's employees have invested in human capital whose value is specific to the goods being produced by the firm. They can keep the firm alive producing these unwanted goods only as long as they are willing to accept wage concessions of a magnitude sufficient to eliminate losses on the sale of the unwanted goods. Most employees will have no large investment in product-specific human capital and will have no objection to a change in the product mix produced by the firm. Indeed, employees may work for a firm honestly and hard but purchase a rival's product in the marketplace. The internal constituency of the firm has little interest and even less say in the product mix offered by the firm. The external constituency determines this in a market-based economy.

The story is different for a political party. The Libertarian Party in the United States continues operating and keeps offering candidates and programs to voters even though these very seldom get elected and acted upon. So does the Socialist Party. These parties are engaged in preference-changing activities more than they are in winning political offices. Their internal constituencies are willing to provide funds and strong efforts only if these parties continue in their attempts to make the preferences of external constituencies more like those of their internal constituencies. External constituencies are not buying, but these parties hope they are listening. If the Libertarian and Socialist Parties were to imitate the major parties, they would lose their party members and need to compete for new members with the major parties. The major political parties, being less doctrinaire than "extreme" parties, have internal constituencies that are more flexible about what programs they want; they are more insistent in seeking power by way of securing political offices. Winning office is not everything for major parties. They do have missionary zeal that makes the programs and candidates they offer unlike those of other major parties. Nonetheless, winning office is much more important to their internal constituencies than it is to parties that are more doctrinaire.

What can we deduce from all this? The mix of output offered by firms is much more in line with what external constituencies want. It is less so for major political parties and much less so for minor, doctrinaire parties. And, in reverse order, the wants and preferences of internal constituencies vary in importance. Dollar "voters" get what they want from the marketplace. Ballot voters get less of what they want and get more of what political internal constituencies want.

There is some exaggeration in the claim just made, but not enough to merit a retraction. Political parties that win office do satisfy the wants of larger constituencies than those that do not win office. The competition to win office influences major political parties and this does bring them closer to offering programs that appeal to larger numbers of voters. However, winning office is a product of two factors: the program (and candidates) offered to voters and the energy and quality of the effort made by a party. The internal constituencies are willing to put more effort into the campaign the more satisfactory to these constituencies are the programs and candidates their party offers to voters. Programs and candidates that win an election are public goods that internal constituencies must live with, so, although they are willing to yield a bit on what their parties stand for, they are not willing to make winning an election the only consideration when they determine how much effort and investment they give to the party. They will accept a somewhat lower probability of winning in return for programs and candidates that are more supportive of what these constituencies want. No political party, even a major political party, completely ignores the preferences of its internal constituency when designing its programs and choosing its candidates. The winning party, unlike the winning firm, gives less attention to what the external constituency wants; a greater difference (than is true for the winning firm) emerges between programs (i.e., products) offered to the external constituency and programs (i.e, products) actually delivered to the external constituency. This effect is made all the stronger because those who lead political parties generally are part of the internal constituency. More important, unlike owners of firms, these leaders do not swallow all the losses their parties sustain when they fail to win. There is no owner of a political party; there is only the team that is the internal constituency. The team, not just the party leader, bears the loss. Because the loss borne by a political leader on failing to win an election is shared broadly, the tendency to cater to internal constituency preferences is all the stronger. It is true, of course, that that the firm's internal constituency bears a part of the losses suffered by an unsuccessful firm, but the much larger part is borne by investor-owners.

The notion that major political parties will compete by formulating programs and choosing candidates that minimize differences between them neglects the implications of such political behavior for the flow of funds and the supply of enthusiastic manpower to these parties. Although the difference between programs and candidates of the Republican and Democratic parties in the United States is not as large as the difference between those of the Libertarians and Socialists, it is nonetheless larger than is suggested by the median voter model.

The contrast with firms in this respect is glaring. A losing firm would very much like to offer a product that is *identical* to that of its most successful rival, and would do so if patent and copyright laws and technical inexperience did not stand in the way. The internal constituencies of rival business firms will not work less hard for a firm if it abandons a somewhat inferior product for one that has all the appearances, as judged by market success, of being a superior product.

If this analysis is not far off the mark, it implies that representative democracy yields outcomes that differ from those based on the assumption that competition between parties results in voter sovereignty. The sovereign group consists of the voters and party members, even if the latter do not vote. What pleases this group will be less than what would please either of its two subparts. This tendency is exacerbated by information cost. Voters are not completely knowledgeable about the programs being offered. And information cost is considerably greater for political activity than for commercial activity. The disincentive for a citizen to invest in knowledge about political programs is high because the programs, being in the nature of public goods, invite citizens to free ride on knowledge that others pay to acquire and because the vote they cast will have an effect on the outcome that is zero for all practical purposes. Neither of these factors is as severe in markets; after all, consumers get what they pay for.

III

Certain realities are explained by all this. Business firms do not inquire into the consumption preferences of their employees. Working hard for the Coca-Cola Corporation does not keep the worker from drinking Pepsi or beer, and the Coca-Cola Corporation does not really care if the worker does not drink Coke frequently. Political parties, however, are prone to vet their internal constituencies to determine if they hold political preferences like those of other members of the internal constituency. A potential worker who holds different political views *is* more likely to work less hard for a party. The higher up the hierarchy of the internal constituency, the more serious is the vetting process. And it becomes even more serious for a political party in power and engaged in selecting people for government employment. Why else have a category of government employees called civil service employees? Why? Well, to protect them from discharge if a party whose programs they do not favor wins office.

Why are political parties not owned? Owners, after discharging contractual obligations to others, enjoy the profit or suffer the loss that remains. Because owners are claimants on this residual, market preferences have considerable leverage over what they can do successfully. An owner of a firm that does what she wants with the firm's assets and not what the market wants quickly loses her wealth. Political parties can remain in the game as long as their internal constituencies are willing to supply effort and funds, and this willingness, since it seeks particular programs as well as offices, can persist through long periods of experiencing defeat at the polls. The imputed loss from these defeats, after all, is not concentrated on party leaders as much as it is concentrated on owners of firms. The assets of the poorly performing firm can be sold to someone who thinks he can alter the product mix to make it more successful. The assets of the poorly performing political party are not concentrated in plant and equipment but in human capital, and this cannot be sold because it is not owned by the party. Even if human capital could be purchased, a new "owner" would not want it, since its psychological makeup is such that it espouses losing causes. There can be no really effective market for control. Someone wishing to mount a political party may as well create one anew. In fact, parties are organized so as to make it difficult to buy them or sell control of them; this is to preserve ideological preferences.[2]

Let us suppose what is probably true, that the wants of external constituencies change through time. Business firms adjust to these changes more quickly because they lack an internal consistency that is highly insistent on continuing old ways. Political parties, on the other hand, possess influential internal consistencies that are willing to accept a lower probability of winning in order to continue marketing programs that appeal to these internal constituencies. This implies greater variation in market share through time for political parties than for business firms. If firms were able to adjust extremely quickly to new external conditions there would be little fluctuation in market share through time. Of course, they cannot change so quickly that this would be true, and so market share will vary. However, the business firm can retain older products

---

[2] Again, I do not wish to overstate the case. The erstwhile mayor of Chicago, Richard Daley, came close to owning the Democratic Party in Chicago land, even to the extent of arranging the succession of control so as to have it eventually pass to his son. However, this is exceptional. Parties sometimes are open for sale. This should be more likely the less ideological is the party, but the transactions that execute the transfer of control will be kept hidden.

for which a market still exists and introduce other, newer products that offer better responses to emerging new trends.

Political parties are tightly tied to existing ideologies and policies, not just because it is important to keep internal constituencies happy but also because it is important to maintain a consistent position. The Democratic Party in the United States has long championed redistribution of wealth. Its internal constituency strongly favors this policy, but even if this is set aside it could not respond quickly or strongly to an increase in the number of effective voters who are wealthy as compared to those who are poor. The attempt to do so would be hampered by the external constituency's doubt that a party engaged in changing its position will hold steady to its promises. It is therefore forced to adopt slow and partial measures to make those changes that it thinks are now more important than they were in the past.. This is especially true because it lacks an owner. No single person's personal fortunes are affected as dramatically by his or her party's failure to keep up with changing times as are the fortunes of owners of firms that fail to keep.

The empirical consequence of all this is that stability in party positions in the face of changing political-economic-demographic conditions will cause large changes in the shares of votes cast for competing parties. The variability of vote share should be larger for competing political parties than is the variability of market share for competing business firms. The variability in the division of votes won by the Democratic and Republican parties in the United States, for example, can be compared to the division of market share won by General Motors and Ford. Consider the period between 1932 and 1964, a period of large changes, from depression to war to prosperous peace. I calculated votes won by the Democratic Party as a percentage of the sum of votes cast for the Democratic and Republican Parties in each year within this period for which there was a presidential election. The standard deviation of these percentages, calculated over the entire period, was 13.13. I also calculated autos sold by General Motors as a percentage of the sum of General Motors and Ford auto sales for years that corresponded to the involved presidential election years. The standard deviation of these percentages across the entire period was only 9.13. The larger variation for political parties may reflect the idiosyncrasy of this single example, but the example shows how the proposition stated above about stability of political party position can be tested.

10 THE PUBLIC CORPORATION: ITS OWNERSHIP AND CONTROL

THE PUBLIC CORPORATION IS, IN A SENSE, CAPITALISM'S answer to the socialist firm. The socialist firm is owned by the state. In concept if not practice, to socialists this means that all citizens are owners. This may be debated when it comes to exercising control over what the socialist firm does, but there is not much to debate about when it comes to bearing the consequences of the firm's operations; all citizens of a socialist country bear some of the cost consequences because they are *compelled* by taxation or other means of government use of resources to share in these costs. The capitalist public corporation is *potentially* "everyone's" firm in that any member of the public (even citizens of nations other than that in which the corporation is based) can purchase shares in its equity; yet, unlike the socialist firm, no one is compelled to do so, and, empirically, it has never been the case that all people do so. The number of independent simultaneous owners of shares, whether persons, joint owners, or institutions, is limited by the number of shares outstanding; however, there is no technically or externally imposed upper limit to the number of shares outstanding, and, since privately organized groups of people can arrange voluntarily to jointly own a share, say through some form of investment club or mutual fund, there really is no upper limit to the number of persons who can have a position in the equity shares of a corporation.

As an institutional type the public corporation has existed for centuries. Economists, however, neglected it until well into the nineteenth century when it rose to prominence in Western economies and when, as a result of Berle and Means's book, *The Modern Corporation and Private Property* (1932), it became a much-debated form of business. The model of the firm that economists had used to help unravel the puzzle of price coordination in a decentralized economy is one that implicitly unites ownership and management into a single "person," a person who makes all decisions about what employees do with the firm's resources on the basis of known technology and known prices. Prices plus technology and profit-maximizing behavior determine all that this firm does. The model, however, does not deal at all with the internal practices of the firm that help its owner achieve his or her objective. Its role is to explicate the role of the price system, not to explore owner-manager tactics, techniques, and strategies.

The absence of a theory that depicts the problems of managing the firm, and that explores the way real firms resolve these problems, drew comments here and there, but it was the Berle and Means book that brought the neglect of these problems to the fore. They did so by stressing the difference between the corporation and the firm that is depicted in the work of the neoclassical economists. The book emphasizes the large number of shareholders of the modern corporation and the relatively small number of shares the typical investor owns. Where the proprietorship seems to unite ownership and control in one person, as does the neoclassical theory of the firm, the corporation disperses ownership across a large number of investors and, in doing so, weakens the ability of shareholders to control what management does. The authors recount through a few examples that this separation seems, at least sometimes, to put management interests before shareholder interests. This was the book's central theme: shareholders, although the legitimate owners of the corporation, are in no position to keep professional management from diverting resources to its own uses. The book caused a stir among lawyers and economists. Legal scholars retained a strong interest in its message, which made corporate law a much more important legal specialty, but economists soon turned to the more serious problems of unemployment and deflation that came with the Great Depression. Economists, with one or two exceptions, did not return to the problem of business organization until World War II ended.

My discussion of the corporation is ordered as follows. The issue of how ownership of the corporation is to be viewed is discussed first; this is followed by discussion of concerns about the separation between ownership and control.

I

The debate among legal scholars about who owns the corporation came of age during the last half-century, during which a "stakeholder" view of the corporation emerged. In its normative application, the stakeholder concept argues that control of what the corporation does with its assets should reside in all parties, or groups, who are affected by the corporation's actions. The usual notion of stakeholders includes shareholders, employees, and creditors, and sometimes even members of the community. Although the implied standard is based on the bearing of consequences from corporate activities, there is no stipulation as to how serious these consequences must be for a person or group to qualify as a stakeholder. Without a limiting stipulation, the standard could apply to those who supply material inputs to the corporation and to those who purchase goods from it. The more inclusive is the notion of a stakeholder, the more the public corporation becomes like the socialist firm, whose stakeholders include the entire citizenry of a nation. Perhaps the popularity of socialism in Europe accounts for the support given there in recent years to the stakeholder view of the corporation.

Although the stakeholder view would seem to be applicable to proprietorships and partnerships as well as to corporations, it is the corporation that has been the prominent subject of reforms and debates. This suggests that the stakeholder view rests on more than just the bearing of consequences. It would also seem to rest on the unique ownership structure of the typical corporation, which, along lines argued by Berle and Means, seems to weaken shareholders' ability to control the corporation in which they own shares. If shareholders cannot control the corporation, and if the directors and management of the corporation, who are stakeholders, can, and do (without at the same time being significant shareholders), well then, why not allow other stakeholders to participate directly in the control process? The other stakeholders that supporters of the stakeholder view have in mind are usually the corporation's employees and the local community in which the corporation's assets are located.

The dominant but not unchallenged view that U.S. courts have taken toward the corporation is that stockholders are the principals of the corporation to whom management, directors, and employees owe loyalty and due diligence. This view is no longer so solidly in place. Many states, for example, have adopted legislation to protect management from corporate takeovers even though shareholders may desire to sell their shares to those seeking to acquire control of the corporation; and legislation recently adopted by Pennsylvania permits board directors to use corporate assets in ways that benefit parties, such as charitable institutions, over the opposition of shareholders. If we were to rely on the judgments of legislatures and courts in the various states, we would conclude that there now is a division of opinion about the appropriateness of the stakeholder view of the corporation. I refrain from entering a debate about what the prevailing legal situation calls for or should call for, leaving this to legal scholars. Instead, let us explore the nature of the corporation in the "raw," under the supposition that its creation and organization is a purely private matter. Doing this establishes a foundation for debate about legal positions.

Armen Alchian and I played an unintended role in the formulation of the stakeholder view of locating rights to control what the corporation does. Our article, "Production, Information Costs, and Economic Organization," published in 1972, depicted the firm (not just the corporation) as a nexus of contracts. Investors contract with potential suppliers, employees, and creditors to bring resources to the task of production. All these parties have an interest in the firm's success, since the terms on which they bring resources to this task are improved if the probability of success is greater. Nonetheless, each party also has a private interest that will sometimes compete with the firm's success. A genuine team effort implies that the isolation of one team member's contribution to the firm is difficult to measure. There then exists a positive probability that shirking by a team member will go undetected. This creates an incentive for individual members of the team to reduce their efforts on behalf of the firm and turn instead to personal matters, relying on other team members to improve the firm's performance. The benefit of shirking is the shirker's alone; the cost is borne by the entire team.

To control shirking, there must be a party who oversees, monitors, and disciplines other members of the team, who provides the overall formulation of the team's goals, and who does so without shirking. The organizational problem is solved by compensating this "central contractor" with the post-operation profit (the "residual" that remains after other participants receive their contractual wage, interest, or rent). This person will be able to collect a larger residual if he or she does a better job of seeing to it that others do their work well. The central contractor cannot shift the cost of any shirking he or she might do to other central contractors, and so there is no incentive for the central contractor to shirk. This arrangement is one that, in principle at least, will be favored by all team members because it maximizes the probability of success for the team; maximizing this probability allows each team member to serve on the team that provides more attractive returns to him or her.

Out of this model of the firm's organization, we are able to rationalize the contractual payments that some team members receive (employees, creditors, landlords) and the residual retention that compensates the central contractor, who usually will have made a substantial contribution of difficult-to-retrieve resources to the firm. This is the person we normally identify as the firm's owner. The central contractor owns the assets he brings to the team effort. These are primarily his human capital and the assets secured by the firm with his funds. (The public corporation makes this identification somewhat more difficult because the firm in this case secures funds from a multitude of shareholders.)

In the case of a proprietorship, there is advantage in making the central contractor the one whose assets are most bound to the nexus of contracts that defines the firm, and also in entitling him or her to the profit residual. These arrangements yield an efficient team organization. They do not preclude delegation of responsibilities and duties to others, but the right to delegate ultimately traces back, possibly through middle management, to the central contractor. Those who have agreed to accept these delegated responsibilities and duties owe due diligence and loyalty to the central contractor even as they use their own judgment to control the way the firm's resources are employed. Such duty and loyalty spring from the nature of contractual obligations. It is necessary to avoid the mistake of confusing control with ownership, since control by those other than the owner has been obtained by delegation from the owner or central contractor.

For the proprietorship, ownership and the source of delegated control are united in *one* person who, as the person who retains the residual, has no incentive to shirk in performing his or her tasks of delegating, monitoring, disciplining, and strategizing. We call this person the owner of the firm, but he or she does not own all the assets that are brought into the nexus of contracts. The human capital the proprietor hires, the capital the proprietor borrows, or the land he or she rents all belong to others who make them available to the team on a contractual basis. Recognition of this fact does not lead us to deny that the proprietor owns the assets that belong to him or her or to the firm.

When it comes to the modern corporation, there is no single person who is the equivalent of the central contractor that for the proprietorship is the entrepreneur-owner. The financial commitments that an owner of a proprietorship would make are made, instead, by the many persons who purchase shares from the corporation, either in its initial distribution of shares to the public or in its later issue of new shares. I stress that this is the only fundamental difference between a corporation and a proprietorship, with the partnership sitting partway between these two organizational forms. This difference necessitates a method for determining what shareholders want and, since they hardly ever all want the same thing, a method for resolving different opinions. It also implies a looser connection between shareholder decisions and the performance of those who have been delegated responsibilities for carrying out these decisions than is likely to be found in the proprietorship. The shareholder group, being large and diverse, cannot perform the tasks of monitoring, disciplining, and setting strategy as effectively as a single proprietor, not just because of the difficulties it faces in maintaining effective communication and coordination among shareholders, but also because the typical shareholder, who owns only a small fraction of outstanding shares, has a personal incentive to shirk when it comes to undertaking efforts to monitor and control the firm's professional management and other employees. Delegation of responsibilities is in order, but in a context in which control by shareholders is less effective than it would be if the central contractor was indeed more centralized.

Before discussing what all this means for ownership of the corporation, I point out at once that there is nothing in the basic nature of the corporation that forces it to adopt a rigid, uniform approach to the problems it faces. If we set aside regulatory restrictions on the way a corporation is set up, nothing prohibits the corporation from selling its shares only to those who commit to owning, say, at least 10 percent of the corporation's total equity; nothing prohibits selling more than one class of shares, only some of which may carry the right to vote; and nothing prohibits the use of a rule of decision making that requires the unanimous agreement of shareholders. None of these bear directly on the distinctive quality of the corporation, which is the many owners of outstanding shares. No doubt, some forms of organization will be more desirable to those who create a corporation, but this is also true of those who create a proprietorship. And some forms will be forced on the corporation by state regulation of the way it is set up and organized. To assess ownership of the corporation in its "natural" state, however, it is necessary to strip away regulatory constraints and allow those who create a corporation to set it up in any way they please. There is much confusion among legal scholars between the natural propensities of corporate organization and the modification of these by state- or court-imposed regulations. To simplify matters, I discuss the corporation as organized on the basis of one share, one vote, and majority control of shareholder decisions, but I ask the reader to remember that this may not reflect the assortment of organizational arrangements that could arise in the absence of regulation. With the "natural" corporation in hand, it is a simple matter to locate ownership.

The proprietor, being solely in control of the resources he commits and secures through contractual arrangements with others, is the owner of the firm because his rights include exclusivity and alienability in regard to the uses that are made of the firm's assets. Other contracting agents have similar rights in the assets they own, but these, by contractual arrangement, are put under the temporary control of the proprietor and the agents he chooses.

In the partnership and the closed corporation, there is a small group of persons who invest in the firm and who share control over the resources they commit and the contracts they offer to other asset owners.[1] Unlike the proprietorship, there must be an agreed procedure by which to reconcile the differing views of the partners; it may be the rule of a majority, or the rule of unanimity; or some other such agreed rule. It will also be true that the agreement as it will be enforced in private cases bars a partner from acting in ways that are knowingly at odds with the success of the partnership. Since it is unlikely that the rule of decision making will allow a single partner to make all decisions (or delegate all decisions) regarding the use of the partnership's resources, including especially the right to alienate these resources, it cannot be said that any one partner owns the partnership. However, in accord with the rule of decision making set up by the partners, it can be said that a subgroup of partners does own the partnership, recognizing that the membership in this subgroup may be different through time and across problems.

The difference between the partnership and the corporation lies in ease of communication between partners, a situation that is brought about by two facts: partners will be fewer in number than shareholders, and the identities of partners will be subject to much less change through time than the identities of persons who become shareholders. This is especially true of the public corporation, which offers shares for sale to all persons and permits the unfettered sale of shares that are owned by the public. No single shareholder can be said to own the corporation; he or she

---

[1] The closed corporation is organized to realize some of the advantages of incorporation without becoming open to public purchase of shares. The advent of legislation that eased the act of creating a public corporation led to the substitution of public corporations for closed corporations, but the latter remain an important form of business organization.

owns shares in the corporation and is privileged to exercise all rights that attach to these shares, including the right to alienate them and to cast votes on issues that come before shareholders. And, like the partnership, it can be said that the owner of the public corporation is a consenting subgroup of shareholders that is large enough to satisfy the rule of decision making that has been adopted (here, a simple majority of votes cast). This subgroup will, of course, be subject to change through time and across issues. Nonetheless, it possesses all the key rights that establish ownership.

Although this discussion identifies the locus of ownership in all three business forms, it makes the decision-making process seem more different than it really is. The partnership and corporation need political-type rules to resolve differences of opinions between, respectively, partners and shareholders. The proprietorship does not, but the proprietor will employ some mental rule of decision making that can be interpreted as the target of the political rules used by partners and shareholders. That is, the proprietor is not always, and probably is never, absolutely sure of the best course to chart for his or her firm or of the best uses to which its resources should be directed. He or she may, for example, list the points in favor of an action and the points in opposition to the action, count the number of points in each list, and give the decision to the list that has the largest number of points, a rule much like the rule of the majority that applies to shareholders. Of course, this is gross simplification of the proprietor's decision-making process, but it will be something like this. The only difference is that the pros and cons are located in the same brain instead of in the brains of different shareholders.

That the rights of a majority of shareholders are those that we use to define ownership does not mean that this (changing) group will be omniscient and omnipotent in its attempts to monitor and discipline management and to develop corporate goals. The ownership structure of the corporation no doubt makes for difficulties in these respects, a fact that makes one wonder why people should bother to own equity shares in a corporation. I answer this question below, but not until I consider in more detail the alleged separation between ownership and control in the corporation.

II

The problem of a separation between ownership and control is thought to be more severe in the corporation than in the proprietorship and partnership because of the diffuse ownership structure of the corporation. This makes communication and action taking more difficult for shareholders. It also makes each shareholder prone to sit back and let other shareholders carry the burdens of monitoring and disciplining the corporation's directors and management team. These difficulties are not present in the proprietorship and are much less severe in the partnership. The posited vacuum of control is thought to be filled by professional management, which, because of decision-making difficulties faced by thousands of shareholders, has been delegated considerable control over the firm's assets.

We may note that there is nothing irrational about this organization, given the costs and errors that will come from a serious effort by shareholders to make detailed business decisions. Most shareholders do not really have any interest in making business decisions, nor do they have the requisite expertise to make those decisions wisely. They will benefit from letting professional managers do this, even if some control must be given to managers to accomplish this. The real issue is not this transfer itself, but the degree to which control is likely to be abused by management. This is usually judged by the degree of diffuseness in the ownership structure of the corporation. Whether the diffuse ownership structure really leads to diversion or misuse of shareholder-owned assets depends on several other considerations. Among these are the substance of corporate bylaws, of wisdom shown by courts in interpreting the bylaws, and the incentives implied by the compensation system used to reward management. And there is the important, but usually neglected, issue relating to the frequency with which significant opportunities arise for management's interest to deviate from shareholder interest, taking into account the value of reputation to management. Clearly, there is much that we do not know about these considerations, and therefore, we are not in a position to pronounce confidently that diffuse ownership of the corporation hurts shareholders very much or very often.

Moreover, if we take a forward-looking view of the problem, people who think about investing in shares of a diffusely owned corporation, anticipating that corporate performance will suffer from self-serving actions of management, will not purchase these shares unless share price is sufficiently low to create an expectation that, after adjusting for poor performance, the investor can expect a competitive rate of return. Quite possibly, the separation of ownership and control is much less damaging to shareholders than is commonly supposed.

However, let us set aside these sources of protection of shareholder interests to discuss ownership structure. This issue is of central importance, not just because the separation between ownership and control has been based on it, but, perhaps more interestingly, because we cannot insulate the corporation and its ownership structure from market forces. If diffuse ownership structure leads to unproductive use of corporate assets, taking account of the advantages of scale and of risk avoidance for shareholders, we should expect the diffusely organized corporation to give way to other business forms and to corporations that are, or have become, less diffuse in their ownership structures. Facts can be brought to bear on this.

The corporation, far from diminishing in importance, has risen to importance on the economic scene. Adam Smith argued in *The Wealth of Nations* (1776) that the joint stock company, the early form of the corporation, could operate effectively only in special circumstances. These included, especially, products that minimized the opaqueness of what was transpiring within the firm; to him this meant something like a utility, whose performance is easier for outsiders to gauge because this involves a single product the amount and value of which can be measured easily by investors. He thought no investor should want to put his funds in a joint stock company more complex than this, because of the difficulties he would face as one of many shareholders in attempting to influence how invested funds are used. History has proved Smith wrong about this, since shareholders have realized after-tax returns on their investments, on average across corporations and through time, that have been on the order of 7 percent to 9 percent. Contrary to what one might suppose from critics of diffuse ownership, the corporation, once an unimportant business form, has become quite important

The ownership structure of the corporation, though much more diffuse than that of the partnership and, of course, than that of the proprietorship, is not so diffuse that shareholders are left without influence over professional management. A study [Demsetz and Lehn (1985)] of the ownership structure of 500 of the largest U.S. corporations, covering the period 1975–80, shows that the five largest shareholding interests controlled, on average, between 25 and 26 percent of outstanding shares. Additionally, this study finds no relationship between accounting measures of profit rates and ownership structure; highly diffuse ownership structures are not negatively associated with profit rates. A more recent study [Holderness (2007)] based on a random sample of U.S. corporations (of *all sizes*), shows that 96 percent of these firms have some shareholders who own large blocks of shares and that, on average, these blockholders own 39 percent of the common stock of their firms. These numbers underestimate the power of the shareholder. Through a variety of devices, such as the adoption of two classes of shares (voting and nonvoting) and the presence of members of the family of a firm's founder on the board of a successor corporation, control is exercised even by persons who own relatively few shares. The gist of all this is that whatever separation between ownership and control there is, it is much less severe than mainline writings on this topic suggest.

Mainline writings are focused on the shift in control to management from shareholders. This shift, I have just argued, has been exaggerated. Ownership structures of corporations are not as diffuse as these writings have assumed. The presence of blockholders in corporate ownership structures gives voice to shareholder interests because, most often, business policies that serve blockholders also will serve minority shareholders, but this is not always true. There are conditions under which the interests of these two groups of shareholders are in conflict. Under these conditions, the influence of blockholders on management decisions may harm minority shareholders. The old view of the separation problem, in which management controls corporations to the detriment of shareholders, gives way to a new view, in which blockholders control corporations to the detriment of minority shareholders. Studies of this new separation problem have not progressed far enough to allow informed discussion of it, but legal and financial scholars already debate it.

Conceptualizing this new view is not straightforward. Supposing the conflict between the two types of shareholder is significant. Why, we may ask, do would-be minority shareholders choose to own shares in corporations in which blockholders have a relevant presence? Obviously, minority shareholders usually do benefit from the ability of blockholders to nullify management misbehavior. But then, those occasions on which blockholders take advantage of minority shareholders may be thought of as minority shareholder compensation of blockholders for undertaking risks, not also borne by minority shareholders, of putting so much wealth into a single firm. After all, blockholders, unlike management, receive no explicit wages for undertaking such risks. Some indirect form of compensating blockholders for the special risks they take on must be found if this means of disciplining management is to be operative; and this means that blockholders need to benefit more from corporate actions than do minority shareholders.[2]

The reader, after comprehending the control problems associated with the public corporation, may well ask why people choose to become corporate shareholders, especially corporate minority shareholders. One reason, of course, is the 7 to 9 percent per annum rate of return that shareholders have earned through historically long periods of time; this beats interest on savings accounts and on many debt instruments, but there are other reasons also. The corporation, like other institutional arrangements, has advantages and disadvantages. It provides an opportunity for an investor to own a highly liquid small equity stake, to have little or no responsibility for actively managing the firm, and to limit losses to the amount paid to acquire the corporation's shares (i.e., limited liability). The high liquidity of investment comes from the large number of shares outstanding, which provides incentives to create and operate organized exchanges on which these shares can be traded. It also comes from the absence of any requirement that management or other shareholders approve sales by a shareholder of the shares he or she owns, a feature of the *public* corporation that is not commonly found in partnerships and closed corporations.

These advantages are implemented in order to avoid problems entrepreneurs and venture capitalists would face when attempting to secure funds from persons who may not be wealthy and who, even if they are wealthy, do not seek to be involved in the running of a firm or in the bearing of high firm-specific risk. The desire to obtain capital from such sources is especially strong if a firm must have very large amounts of capital to compete successfully.

Capitalism itself provides means for reducing the severity of the governance problems that come with the corporation organization.

---

[2] See Demsetz (1986) for an analytical and statistical study of the role of insider trading as a form of differential.

Three disciplining forces may be discussed here: (1) stock prices and hostile takeovers, (2) market institutions that provide information about management competence, and (3) capital markets that give investors a wide variety of ownership structures from which they may choose.

Severe agency problems depress a corporation's stock price. This makes it possible for investor-entrepreneurs to profit from uncovering situations in which agency problems are severe and remedying them, sometimes by way of hostile takeovers. During the decades of the 1980s and 1990s, hostile takeovers in the United States had a profound effect on business organization. The 1980s marked the beginning of a strong response to the management entrenchment problems that had emerged after the Korean War. Over half of all major U.S. corporations became targets of hostile takeover bids early in the 1980s, and many other corporations restructured just to keep from becoming a target. The takeover movement was so successful that managements of the largest U.S. corporations began to petition state governments for protection from corporate "raiders." The battle between the transforming force of markets and the conserving force of politics is evident here.

Market institutions that provide information about the quality of management are an aid to the process of price adjustment but are distinct from it. The Institutional Shareholder Services (ISS), for example, offers information and advice to institutional investors regarding corporate governance quality. A poor ranking can be transformed into a good ranking if a corporation alters its governance arrangements to accord with the standards used by the ISS.

The most important protection of investors comes from competition between alternative investment options. This allows investors to search across corporations to find the combination of good governance and greater liquidity of investment that meets investor preferences. The quality of governance generally will be better if ownership structure is not diffuse, but the liquidity of investments, because there are fewer shareholders, generally will be worse. Investors face a choice between good governance and less liquidity on one hand, and poor governance and more liquidity on the other hand. The variety of investments offered to investors properly includes categorically different investments, such as bonds, mutual funds, savings accounts, and real estate, but in this essay, to retain a focus on the corporation, this variety also includes differences in the degree of diffuseness of corporate ownership structures. The rich variety of corporate ownership structures provides a significant means by which the real cost of misgovernance is reduced for investors. Investors who, because of wealth, psychology, and personal obligations, find misgovernance very costly are able to reduce the probability of bearing this cost; investors of a different sort, who do not find misgovernance so costly, can increase the probability of enjoying very liquid markets for their investments.

Beyond these market forces is the regulation of the corporation, an aspect of the world of corporations that has largely been ignored in this essay. Regulation includes state licensing requirements and legislation such as Sarbanes-Oxley. I do not pursue these here. They have been discussed amply by others. However, regulations of a different sort are not yet widely acknowledged. I refer to tax policy, insider trading policy, antitrust law, and so on. I briefly discuss some of these to conclude this essay.

A tax levied on corporate profit reduces the care and effort owners will put into its operation, since part of the return that would have been received by owners will go to the state. De facto, private owners of the corporation are saddled with a shirking partner, the state, which takes part of the revenue and provides none of the effort to improve the firm's return. Consequently, the greater is the corporate tax rate, the greater the incentive for corporate owners and management to pursue the "quiet life."

A country's policy toward wealth distribution will affect firm size. Large firms in countries that strive to create an egalitarian distribution of wealth will suffer more severe management control problems because equity supplied to such firms will need to come from larger numbers of less wealthy investors, each of whom is likely to purchase a smaller share of corporate equity. The ownership structure of corporations is thereby made more diffuse for any given size of firms. In the absence of state-owned firms or state-granted subsidies, this implies that firm size will be smaller on average than in countries in which there is greater tolerance of wealth inequality, and this implies less ability to take advantage of large-scale production.

Shareholders who have large stockholdings in a single corporation are strongly motivated and better able to monitor and control management than are minority shareholders. The presence of blockholders reduces the degree to which management is entrenched. However, blockholders are burdened with greater firm-specific risk than are minority shareholders; they also are burdened with greater involvement in the corporation's policies and business practices. There is no reward for bearing the special costs that come with a blockholder's stake if all shareholders receive the same return on the investments they make. Hence, if the supply of blockholder investors is to be increased there must be a means of differentiating between them and minority shareholders in terms of return received on investments made. This means does not seem to exist. Large and small shareholdings receive the same dividend per share owned and, for shares bought or sold at the same time, receive or pay the same price.

However, the needed differential return could come to blockholders in the form of access to inside information, the provision of access being a response of management to the voting strength of blockholders. The degree of access, moreover, will correlate with the size of the ownership stake taken by an investor. Insider information enables blockholders to better time trading in their company's stock and in the stocks of firms that supply goods to it and that purchase goods from it. In this way, they receive compensation for bearing firm-specific risk. The greater are the restrictions and penalties applied to insider trading, the smaller is the incentive to become a blockholder. As a result, the separation of control between management and shareholders will be more severe. Minority investors thus face a trade-off – a more effectively run corporation in combination with greater reliance on insider trading to compensate blockholders or a less effectively run corporation with less reliance on insider trading to compensate blockholders. There is no reason to suppose that they would prefer one "corner" solution over the other.

11 CROSSING DISCIPLINARY BOUNDARIES

I FIND SOME JUSTIFICATION IN THE EARLIER ESSAYS ON SELFISH gene theory, the late arrival of capitalism, and Malthus's population trap for finishing this volume with an essay that departs from the volume's emphasis on human behavior and economic institutions. Here, I comment on interdisciplinary work, giving attention to the condition that makes for success in interdisciplinary work and to the different treatments given to competiton by biology and economics. However, when it comes down to it, this last essay does have a place in the general themes of this book. The academic/scientific specialist, after all, is a member of *Homo economicus*.

Adam Smith, the father of modern economics, did deal with our topic in *The Wealth of Nations* (1776), which opens with a discussion of the considerable advantages of specialization. In addition to pointing out the gains in productivity obtainable by relying on specialization, he expressed concerns about what kind of person would emerge from occupations that were intensely specialized. He thought this person would be dull and narrow minded, and he hoped that measures would be taken by society to ameliorate these characteristics. He worried needlessly; increased productivity has allowed for reduction in the hours spent at work, and it has enabled people to engage in other activities, such as travel and reading, that often are quite broadening. And he neglected the advice he gave to policy makers – that they should not imagine that people can be moved about like chess pieces. We have a desire to explore, and we do not always deny this desire in the cause of specialization.

Although intense and diverse today, interdisciplinary work involving economics is not an entirely new phenomenon. Darwin, writing in the nineteenth century, for example, drew on ideas he found in the eighteenth-century works of Smith and Malthus. Rousseau, Hobbes, and Hume were not ignorant of economic writings of their times, nor was Adam Smith ignorant of the ideas of these political philosophers. However, success does not accompany all interdisciplinary efforts, and I offer here a condition for success that is somewhat different from that which has been offered by others.

I

Economists who have been at the forefronts of interdisciplinary efforts have offered very brief observations about why these efforts have been successful. Gary Becker (1976), for example, attributes the successes of economics to the relentless and unflinching application of the "combined assumptions of maximizing behavior, market equilibrium, and stable preferences." Jack Hirshleifer (1985, p. 53) offers a slightly different version of the sources of success:

What gives economics its imperialist invasive power is that our analytical categories – scarcity, cost, preferences, opportunities, etc. – are truly universal in applicability. Even more important is our structured organization of these concepts into the distinct yet intertwined processes of optimization on the individual decision level and equilibrium on the social level of analysis.

Tools of economics and the view economists bring to problems are what these leaders stress, but I argue in the first half of this essay in favor of a different source of successful interdisciplinary work – commonality between the central problems that guided the independent development of the interacting disciplines. Lack of commonality stands as a barrier to successful interaction, even if the interacting disciplines bring quality tools and insightful perspectives to a problem. The concepts and tools peculiar to a discipline owe their existence to the problems the discipline has sought to resolve. Finally, tailored concepts and tools from one discipline will not be of much help to another discipline if the problems these disciplines address are quite different. Much of the successful interaction between law and economics, for example, has its source in common concerns about problems of ownership and contract. And, as I will argue in the second half of this essay, the views taken toward competition in biology and economics differ significantly because the central concerns of the two disciplines differ.

Even those who are not so enthusiastic about interdisciplinary work miss the importance of commonality of problems to interdisciplinary success. R. H. Coase (1978), whose work, though not intentionally, played a large part in creating the common field of law and economics, observes that practitioners of disciplines with which economists attempt to interact know facts that are difficult for the economists, being outsiders, to know unless they give much time and effort to the task of learning, but practitioners of the other field, in contrast, can easily learn the theories that economists bring to them. Accordingly, the services of economists soon become unneeded in the invaded disciplines. This claim is based on specialized knowledge in the two disciplines, but it fails to recognize that this specialization arises from the sort of problems practitioners in the two fields investigate. It also is a claim about the staying quality of *economists* in other disciplines and not about the longevity and impact of their tools and methods. These may have lasting effects even after the delivering messengers have returned to their home disciplines.

Alfred Marshall also has voiced pessimism about border crossing. He discusses interdisciplinary work in Appendix C of his *Principles*

(1890) titled "The Scope and Method of Economics." His central claim is the following:

Economics has made greater advances than any other branch of the social sciences, because it is more definite and exact than any other. But every widening of its scope involves some loss of this scientific precision; and the question of whether the loss is greater than the gain resulting from its greater breadth of outlook, is not to be decided by any hard and fast rule. (p. 780)

He implicitly seems to be discouraging interdisciplinary work because of the deleterious effects he sees this as having on economics itself, not because interacting disciplines will fail to succeed in solving the problems they jointly attack. Marshall describes the strength of economics in terms of its greater definiteness and exactness, but he does not note that a difference in this strength for two interacting disciplines may in fact derive from the differences in the problems that are central to them.

II

The problem that has been most important to economists when economics matured into a social science has been described more than once in earlier essays in this volume. It is to understand how a complex, decentralized economic system brings forth an allocation of resources that seems to have sensible properties. I note here one important empirical aspect of this economic task. It is set mainly in the context of markets, exchange, and commercial dealings. Smith's *Wealth of Nations* (1776), Ricardo's *Political Economy and Taxation* (1817), Miles's *Principles of Political Economy* (1929), Marshall's *Principles of Economics* (1890), and Pigou's *Economics of Welfare* (1920) are all focused on this problem and, to a large extent, on this context. The world of markets and commerce gave economists data, commensurable measures of economic activity – prices, quantities of goods, profits, and costs.[1] It is this focus that made it easier for economics to achieve the higher state of definiteness and exactness to which Marshall referred. It also guided the development of tools and concepts. The model and tools developed to understand decentralization, applied to a data-rich setting, made progress in economics rapid in comparison with the other social sciences. Interaction between economics and another discipline is unlikely to be very productive if the problems important to the two disciplines differ in substance, and it is even less likely to be successful if the other discipline involves settings that do not readily lend themselves to quantitative measurement.

III

The decentralization puzzle has not been focused on by other social sciences during their developmental periods. This should come as no surprise. That we even have a collection of distinct disciplines is due to the different problems they address. The interactions between economics and biology and between economics and history have been most active during periods when the problems studied were much more like each other. Mainly, this means a shared interest in change through time. These periods in economics are those that we call classical and contemporary. The thinking of neoclassical economists, in contrast, was dominated by the attempt to formalize a solution to the spontaneous order puzzle, a problem that they approached in static terms. Classicalists gave and contemporary economists give much more attention to economic development and stability of development. The attention of economists during the first half of the twentieth century, marked as it was by great wars and the Great Depression, was brought to what came to be known as macroeconomic problems. The main concern of these

---

[1] Only personal "utility" was beyond direct measurement, but it was treated as determinable in an ordinal sense that accorded with revealed preferences.

was one of change through time. And this would bring economics back to an earlier concern of the classical economists with material progress, a concern for which the static model developed by neoclassicalists to understand spontaneous order is ill-equipped to handle.

Neoclassical economists also neglected two problems that became important late in the nineteenth and early in the twentieth centuries. The first is the problem of monopoly. Neoclassical economists did model the monopoly firm, but they did not treat it as an important social phenomenon. Usually they confined discussion of monopoly to the footnotes of a text that mainly wrestled with the formulation and consequences of a perfectly decentralized economy. The populist movements in the United States during the 1920s and 1930s made the monopoly problem important enough to marshal support for and to obtain passage of the Act to Regulate Transportation (1887) and the Sherman Antitrust Act (1890). These important laws drew the interests of legal scholars and economists in the United States into much closer proximity than was true during the neoclassical period.

This bond became still tighter during the 1930s, when problems of the business firm became more important. Neoclassical economists had pushed the firm into the background as they developed the tools of supply and demand and sought to understand the impersonal setting of prices on markets. The means by which an owner of a firm managed to put the resources under his or her control to uses that maximized profit went unexamined during the neoclassical period. The firm was modeled as a unit of production that was controlled by its owner who, in ways unspecified by neoclassical economists, somehow achieved maximum profit. The neglect of the inner workings of the firm attracted attention here and there, but the topic did not become important to the work of economists until well after World War I. By that time, the public corporation had risen to new heights of importance in the economic system, and it attracted the attention and pens of Berle and Means, one a lawyer and the other an economist. Their book, *The Modern Corporation and Private Property* (1932), awakened economists and legal scholars to what the authors perceived to be the serious problem of a separation between ownership and control.

Unlike the firm of neoclassical theory, in which full control is simply presumed to be exercised by a firm's owner, the corporation, with its ownership divided across thousands of equity shareholders, seemed to have no internal linking of ownership and control. Berle and Means claimed that control had shifted from owners of the firm to professional managers, who need not be, and often were not, significant holders of equity shares. Their work not only energized corporate law, it also drew the attention of economists to the inner workings of the firm; again, a unifying of interests.

A third unifying force blossomed during the last half of the twentieth century, as a result of R. H. Coase's (1960) attack on the doctrinal perception economists held toward the externality problem that had been highlighted in the work of A. C. Pigou during the first decade of that century. A side effect of Coase's work was to make economists aware of another neglect of neoclassical economics. It had developed its model of perfect decentralization by assuming implicitly, but not at all by discussing, the existence of a functioning private property system. Private ownership of resources, Coase argued, would eliminate the externality problem, at least if the cost of using the price system was zero. The questions of how to define private property and how to explain its existence became important and were attended to by economists familiar with Coase's work. Legal scholars had wrestled with problems of property law for some time, but without a theory of property, and so, once again, we had a joining of the interests of these two disciplines.

As a result of the importance now attached to monopoly, to the inner workings of the firm, and to private ownership of resources, the new interdisciplinary field – law and economics – came to life. This probably is the most successful interactive effort to date that involves economics.

Other examples can be noted. Sociology and economics have a common interest that runs the gamut between quality of labor, education of people, and criminal behavior. G. S. Becker's (1976) work on human capital gave these interests a common theoretical base. The resulting interaction between the two disciplines continues strong, although I think it has not yet spawned a new field of economic sociology.

Other instances of commonality with problems of economics may be cited. Anthropologists have had a long-standing interest in modes of exchange among primitive peoples, and economics, almost from its inception, has been interested in exchange. Economic work on equilibrium and biological work on evolutionarily stable equilibrium have an important commonality. Darwin's work on natural selection was influenced by Smith's discovery of the hidden hand of competition and by Malthus's work on the effect that population change has on living standards. However, the speciation problem, so central to biology since Darwin wrote, seems to have no commonality with the spontaneous order problem that was so important to economics. And, although the work of Schumpeter on business cycles and development is suggestive, economics does not yet seem to have prominent interests that share commonality with biological interests in genetic inheritance and random mutations. Perhaps this will change. The timing of occurrences of commonality in problems in biology and economics explains the early interaction between Darwinians and the writings of classical economists and the absence of active interaction between biologists and the writings of neoclassical economists.

The most important commonality between biological and economic interests today arises from the concern of both disciplines with behavior. Organism behavior presumably is a product of natural selection, and this makes it tie into the speciation problem. While economics takes the human species as a given and therefore has no direct interest in speciation, it does have an interest in the fact that behavior may be equated to wants. Economists have found it necessary, since the birth of their discipline, to take human wants as unexplained givens. Biology offers to economics an explanation of the origin of wants; natural selection has disfavored organisms possessed of wants that are incongruous with survival needs and favored organisms possessed of wants that help to meet the test of survival. The biological view gives a substance to human wants that the economic view, in simply taking wants as exogenous, does not.

A major conceptual objective of neoclassical economics has been to determine the defining conditions of the mix of goods that will be an outcome of the operations of a decentralized economic system. Political scientists have long been concerned about the mix of legislation that will be produced by the electoral process and the legislatures that act as agents for those who elect them. This commonality of interests made for a very useful interaction between the two disciplines, largely initiated in two strains of work by economists. Buchanan and Tullock (1962) disaggregated legislatures into individually acting legislators and devised imaginative methods, such as "log rolling," by which these legislators could negotiate with each other. Stigler (1971) viewed regulators as if they were firms, selling their services to the industries being regulated and receiving compensation from these industries through support for appointment and reelection. These two approaches led to an outpouring of meaningful work in both disciplines about the legislative process.

The point of these examples is to show that many, if not most, successful interactions with economics have occurred in the presence of commonality between the interests of the interacting disciplines, a condition that differs from one that equates success to the superiority of the concepts and tools of economics. Such successes do not necessarily result in a merged, new discipline. It usually will be the case that much that is not held in common remains in two interacting disciplines, and this is likely to keep them fairly well specialized to deal with their own problems. As a case in point, let us consider differences between the way competition is treated by biologists and economists.

IV

Competition, in common usage, usually refers to rivalrous inter-action between people or groups of people. While this is not incon-sistent with the ways in which competition is viewed by biologists and economists, it is not broad enough to match their views; they interpret use of the same scarce resources by different people, orga-nizations, or organisms as competition even if conscious rivalrous behavior is not involved. One person's use of a scarce resource usually implies that less of the resource is available to others; this "zero sum" relationship, whether it does or does not involve rival-rous intents, establishes a competitive relationship as this is meant in these two disciplines.

Although biologists and economists are in agreement in this respect, their views of competition differ in other regards. Biolo-gists view competition as an ever-present condition in nature if rel-evant resources are scarce. Competition to biologists is constantly at work in shaping organism survival probabilities. Economists, however, think of competition as either strong or weak and possi-bly even as completely absent. This seems a bit odd if competition is thought to be implied by scarce resources. The monopolist, for example, is defined as a producer that is not subjected to competi-tion, and this is so even though a firm that has become a monopolist simply bested rivals in seeking buyers for its product or protective legislation. The long-held belief of economists that the last firm standing in a market can keep price above cost is incorrect precisely because it is based on neglect of how this firm actually bested rivals in what we may presume was a competitive struggle. Competition from producers of other goods is a major source of the inverse relationship that links a rise in the price of the monopolist's good to a reduction in the quantity of the good sold by the monopolist.

If this mischaracterizes the true view of economists, who know full well that the monopolist is not completely without some competitive pressure, it does not mischaracterize their belief that the intensity of competition is not only variable but that it is also subject to human control, a belief not held, or, at least not thought important, by biologists. A comparison of the economic models of markets, that we know as perfect competition, monopolistic competition, oligopoly, and monopoly, so often used and discussed in economics, clearly illustrates the belief of economists about the variable and controllable nature of competitive intensity. A market whose underlying conditions change, or are changed, from those of perfect competition to those of monopoly and points between is perceived to have undergone marked changes in competitive intensity. That this change is also believed subject to human control is especially visible in writings about historical events and public policy. The "robber barons" of economic folklore are thought to have, through foresight and effort, personally transformed highly competitive markets into resilient monopolized markets. This belief is partly the source of the Sherman Antitrust Act, the core of U.S. antitrust policy. The Act is clearly premised on the ability of policy to control competitive intensity. Sections 1 and 2 of the Act call upon the Justice Department and the broader legal system to make

... every contract, combination in the form of trust or otherwise, or conspiracy, in restraint of trade or commerce among the several States, or with foreign nations, ... illegal.

And to make every person

... who shall monopolize, or attempt to monopolize any part of the trade or commerce among the several States, or with foreign nations ... guilty of a felony.

Analogous beliefs are not prominent in biology. It is difficult even to find biological writings that center on a concept, or even refer to it tangentially, like that of economic monopoly; similarly for the notion of different degrees of competitive intensity. The conditions that confer competitive advantage may vary, but not the intensity of competition within these conditions. This is generally true even though biological situations are discussed that would seem to imply, to economists at least, a reduction in competitive intensity. I offer examples of two such situations, one involving personalized rivalry and the second involving non-rivalrous multi-organism use of the same scarce resources.

(1) Through successful combat with rivals, a male sea lion achieves the status of beach master, acquiring thereby privileged access to resident female sea lions. This privilege, as an imperfectly accepted sea lion custom, offers the beach master a measure of protection from rival seekers of access to female sea lions, but it is not viewed as weakened competition by biologists. Instead, they see it as an integral part of an intensely competitive natural selection process that assigns different probabilities to the survival of the genes of different male sea lions.

(2) A species stumbles into a nutritionally abundant new source of food. Discoverers of this niche, for a time, are its sole occupiers. It offers them a supply of food so large that consumption by any one of the discovers, or even by all of them, does not make the food a scarce resource. Competition is absent or weak. Ultimately, of course, propagation by the niche's discoverers and the entry of outsiders succeeds in transforming the available food supply into a scarce resource.

Again, as in the case of a beach master sea lion, they view the entire process, from discovery of the niche to its subsequent occupation by offspring and outsiders, as part of the continuing competitive process implicit in natural selection. Biologists would have great difficulty viewing cases such as these as they might be viewed by economists. If they did so, they would be compelled to contemplate the possibility of an end to evolution.

Biologists similarly do not endow people with much power to affect the intensity of competition, but people obviously do have some control of the manner in which competition affects species. Selective breeding and genetic engineering do affect the way in which competition manifests itself, but biologists see these either as empirically unimportant or as ways to affect the way competition manifests itself rather than as controlling the intensity of competition itself. Thus, Darwin, on page 115 of *The Origin of Species*, writes:

Owing to this struggle for life, any variation, however slight, . . . if it be in any degree profitable to an individual of any species . . . will tend to the preservation of that individual, and will generally be inherited by its offspring. The offspring also will thus have a better chance of surviving . . . I have called this principle . . . Natural Selection, in order to mark its relation to man's power of selection. We have seen that man by selection can certainly produce great results. . . . But Natural Selection . . . is a power incessantly ready for action, and is as immeasurably superior to man's feeble efforts, as the works of Nature.

The predominant biological view, from Darwin to present times, makes speciation the provenance of uncontrollable and exogenously determined "natural" conditions.

v

An important source of the differences between these views toward competition is the difference in the central problems that guided development of these disciplines during their formative years. As has been noted more than once in earlier essays, the historically important central puzzle of economics was to explain how independently acting people in an unplanned, decentralized, private ownership economic system allocate their resources and, in particular, to explain how it is that the uses they seem to make of resources seem to be well coordinated. Corn and other agricultural products are planted and harvested by many such people, none of whom coordinate their production plans with others. Their products are used by a multitude of potential purchasers, none of whom coordinate their purchasing plans. Furthermore, producers, as a group, do not communicate with purchasers, as a group. Yet, the quantities of these products brought to market are in approximate agreement with quantities that users of these products desire to secure. Shortages and surpluses of goods are generally very small percentages of total outputs. How does this happen? What are the social consequences for the prices and quantities that make this happen? Much of the work of biologists during the post-Darwin history of their discipline has been guided by the speciation puzzle. This is to explain the multiplicity of life forms and evidence of their apparent modification through time. There is no obvious similarity between this puzzle and that which economists sought to resolve.

An economic puzzle similar to the biological puzzle might ask why we observe a multiplicity of goods and why the nature and form of these goods have changed through time. In fact, economists found it convenient to model the decentralized economy by taking human wants, available goods, and production technologies as exogenous givens, not as changing through time. Decentralization is a phenomenon unto itself. It is independent of specific preferences for goods and of changes in these and in technologies through time, so why complicate the study of decentralization by burdening it with questions relating to the number of goods and to changes in tastes and technologies? Holding this set of variables constant, economists were able to focus on the coordination problem embedded in a decentralized economic system.

The two puzzles, however, do share a common core in that both seek to uncover processes that affect patterns of outcomes, resource allocation in economics and life forms in biology. Both disciplines sought to resolve the puzzle that is created by treating these processes as unplanned by a central planner or God. Economists found their process in markets and the price system. Biologists found theirs in natural selection and the inheritability of genes. Both processes, it may be noted, derive their relevance from the fact that resources are scarce. All people cannot have all the goods or resources they desire; all organisms cannot have all the resources that facilitate survival. Both disciplines also take the active unit to be the individual, whether person or organism. Beyond these important similarities, important differences remain.

Biology imposes no constraints on how organisms succeed or fail in the survival game. All tactics and strategies are acceptable, some of which might be thought of by economists and others as weakening competition. The sea lion that becomes beach master gains control of a beach for a period of time, thereby, to some extent, (not quite) monopolizing the attention of resident female sea lions, but viewed in the context of the speciation problem this becomes a competitive strategy that impacts gene quality and gene survival. It is easy to see why biologists have little use for attaching significance to a concept like monopoly or for thinking of competition as more or less intense.

In contrast to biology, available strategies are necessarily restricted in the context of the puzzle that economists sought to resolve. The pure decentralized, private ownership economic system does, after all, require decentralization and private ownership. For ownership to be private, competitive strategies such as theft and violence must be barred from the analysis, since their presence would undermine the meaning of private ownership. Decentralization also rules out strategies and capabilities (i.e., scale economies) that allow some to acquire influence over price and who, by setting price, can influence decisions made by others. Possession or acquisition of market shares large enough to allow firms or their owners to influence market prices convey the power to influence decisions and actions taken by others. To allow strategies that create this situation would transform the study of decentralization into a study in the exercise of conscious control by some over the activities of others.

These limitations on strategies and tactics, though necessary if the characteristics of a spontaneous economic order are to be maintained, led economists to interpret the violations of these limitations as creating imperfections in competition. This interpretation confused restraints necessary to establish a spontaneous order puzzle and restraints necessary to establish a perfectly competitive order. Perfect decentralization and perfect competition, whatever the latter might mean, came to be confused with each other, and conditions that violated perfect decentralization came to be confused with those that violated perfect competition.

The source of this confusion is found in the modeling of the price system. Prices must be taken as givens by both buyers and sellers if people in a perfectly decentralized economy are unable to influence decisions made by others; hence, the necessity for price-taker behavior. There then began a search for the necessary and sufficient conditions which, if stipulated, implied price-taker behavior. A lack of ability to control price through personal actions, a necessary condition of perfect decentralization, came to be confused with a necessary condition for competition. Tactical and strategic maneuvers to influence price, all of which would be thought of as competitive acts by biologists, came to be viewed by economists as inconsistent with fully competitive conditions.

I make no brief here for or against policies whose intent is to make the economy conform more closely to the conceptualization of a perfectly decentralized economic system. My claim is only that the effect of violations of these restrictions are misconceived to be the undermining of competition when, in fact, they undermine perfect decentralization. And, moreover, to insist on price-taker behavior is to rule out active price competition.

The Sherman Act, while in the process of becoming law, was favored by some economists and opposed by others. Clearly involved in this debate was a notion of a "desirable" or "preferred" state of the economy, and embedded within this was a normative approach to competition. Biologists have not completely avoided normative involvement, especially in regard to selective breeding, eugenics, genetic engineering, and, in contemporary times, global warming, although the degree of their involvement has been much less than economist involvement in public policies. However, biologists have taken no normative position toward competition, toward one competitive tactic over another, or toward one pattern of evolved life forms over another. One source of this difference between economists and biologists also is found in the central puzzles of the two disciplines.

The speciation puzzle did not contain within it a viable normative problem. It was a problem in pure explanation, like the problem of explanation sought by physicists. Of course, in the background, there was a hotly debated issue about the necessity of bringing religion and God into the solution to the speciation problem. This was partly conducted on scientific grounds. Which of these two views best explained the evidence then being uncovered? But this was not a debate between biologists about whether natural selection should be thought of in normative terms; it was not about whether one pattern of evolution was or is better than another. In economics, an important economic debate was and is about whether one form of economic organization is better or worse than another form. Capitalism or socialism? And in economics, such debate extended to preferences for one form of competition over another.

This difference between the disciplines is, I believe, a necessary outcome of the spontaneous order problem that shaped economics, for "order" is thought to be better than chaos. The newly emerged economic system that classical and neoclassical economists sought to explain presented an interesting puzzle precisely because it seemed to yield an allocation of resources that was in important respects desirable. From its very inception, then, economics became enmeshed in normative considerations. And these, for reasons given above, ultimately led to the anointing of some competitive activities and market conditions as more desirable than others. (It is, of course, necessary to point out that income flows to those who are capable debaters about which policies are good for society and which are not.)

The speciation puzzle pursued by biologists, in contrast, does not present a normative issue involving order and chaos. It presents puzzles about the number of different life forms and the changing characteristics of these through time. Biologists make no claim that the pattern of outcomes that arise from natural selection at one time in the history of life is any better or worse than the pattern of outcomes that arise at another time. They do claim that the environmental conditions that produced one of these outcomes were better than the environmental conditions that produced other outcomes. And they do not claim that some natural forces that create mutants are preferred to others.

If economists had taken on the puzzle of how a decentralized economy allocates resources without, at the same time, distinguishing orderly from disorderly outcomes, their discipline might have matured without the considerable attention it has given to normative evaluation of means and outcomes. It is difficult to see how this judgment-neutral approach could have been pursued, since economics emerged from normative claims about policy toward social organization. We might still be waiting for a book like Smith's *Wealth of Nations* if he had not been arguing with mercantilists about how *well* mercantilism suits mankind's *needs* as compared with relatively uncontrolled markets.

REFERENCES

Alchian, A. A., and Demsetz, H. (1972) Production, information costs, and economic organization. *Amer Econ Rev* 62(5): 777–95.

Allen, G. C. (1929) *The Industrial Development of Birmingham and the Black Country, 1860–1927* (London: George Allen and Unwin).

Becker, G. S. (1976) *The Economic Approach to Human Behavior* (Chicago: Univ. of Chicago Press).

Berle, A. A., and Means, C. G. (1932) *The Modern Corporation and Private Property*. (New York: Macmillan).

Buchanan, James M., and Tullock, Gordon (1962) *The Calculus of Consent* (Ann Arbor: Univ. of Michigan Press).

Coase, Ronald H. (1937) The nature of the firm. *Economica* 4(16): 386–405.

Coase, Ronald H. (1959) The Federal Communications Commission. *J Law Econ* 2:1–40.

Coase, Ronald H. (1960) The problem of social cost. *J Law Econ* 3(1): 1–44.

Coase, Ronald H. (1978) Economics and contiguous disciplines. *J Legal Stud* 7: 201–11.

Dawkins, Richard (1976; 2nd ed. 1989) *The Selfish Gene* (Oxford: Oxford Univ. Press).

Demsetz, H. (1964) The exchange and enforcement of property rights. *J Law Econ* 7(Oct.): 11–26.

Demsetz, H. (1967) Toward a theory of property rights. *Amer Econ Rev* LVII(2): 347–59.

Demsetz, H. (1968) The cost of transacting on the New York Stock Exchange. *Quart J Econ* 82(1): 33–53.

Demsetz, H. and Lehn, K. (1985) The structure of corporate ownership: causes and consequences. *J Pol Econ* 93(6): 1155–77.

Demsetz, H. (1986) Corporate control, insider trading, and rates of return. *Amer Econ Rev* 76(2): 313–16.

References

Demsetz, H. (1997) The primacy of economics: An examination of the comparative success of economics in the social sciences. *Econ Inquiry*: 1–11.

Diamond, J. (1997) *Guns, Germs, and Steel* (New York: W. W. Norton).

Downs, Anthony (1957) *An Economic Theory of Democracy* (New York: Harper and Row).

Frank, Robert H. (1999) *Luxury Fever* (Princeton, N.J.: Princeton Univ. Press).

Galbraith, John K. (1958) *The Affluent Society* (Boston: Houghton Mifflin).

Galbraith, John K. (1967) *The New Industrial State* (Boston: Houghton Mifflin).

Hardin, Garrett (1968) The tragedy of the commons. *Science* 162: 1243–8.

Hayek, Friedrich A. von (1988) *The Fatal Conceit* (Chicago: Univ. of Chicago Press).

Hirshleifer, Jack. (1985) The expanding domain of economics. *Amer Econ Rev* 75(6): 53–68.

Holderness, Clifford G. (2007) The myth of diffuse ownership in the United States. *Rev. Finan. Stud.* Advance Access.

Knight, Frank H. (1921) *Risk, Uncertainty, and Profit* (Republished 1965, New York: Harper & Row).

Lal, D. (2006) *Reviving the Invisibile Hand* (Princeton: Princeton University Press).

Maine, Henry (1861 ed.) *Ancient Laws* (London: Pollock).

Marshall, Alfred (1890) *Principles of Economics* (8th ed., Macmillan; New York, 1948; 1st ed., 1890).

Pigou, A. C. (1920) *The Economics of Welfare* (London: Macmillan).

Ridley, Matt (1996) *The Origin of Virtue* (New York: Penguin Books).

Rogers, A. R. (1995) Genetic evidence for a pleistocene population explosion. *Evolution* 49(August): 608–15.

Schumpeter, J. A. (1939) *Business Cycles* (New York: McGraw-Hill).

Schumpeter, J. A. (1950) Capitalism, Socialism, and Democracy (New York: Harper and Brothers).

Smith, Adam (1776) *The Wealth of Nations* (Chicago: University of Chicago Press ed. 1976; Cannon ed., originally published by Methuen & Co., Ltd. 1904).

Stigler, George J. (1971) The theory of economic regulation. *Bell J Econ* 2(1): 3–21.

Veblen, Thorstein (1973) *The Theory of the Leisure Class* (Boston: Houghton Mifflen Co. Originally published 1899).

Whybrow, Peter C. (2005) *American Mania, When More Is Not Enough* (New York: W. W. Norton).

INDEX

Accumulation of assets
  agricultural society, in, 70
  capitalism, as fundamental element of,
    81–82
  primitive man, impracticability for,
    67
Act to Regulate Transportation, 165
Advertising, 132
Agency problems in corporations, 156
Agricultural society, 68–72
  accumulation of assets in, 70
  advances, effect of, 70
  decline of, 76–77
  enclosure, 70–71
  excess product, effect of, 73
  mobility, reduced need for, 69–70
  overview, 68–69
  private ownership rights in, 71–72
  settlement, rise of, 69–70
  specialization, effect of, 73
Alchian, Armen A., 145
Allen, C. C., 16
Allocation of resources. *See* Efficient
  allocation of resources
Altered genes, 43–44
Altruistic behavior
  biological closeness, effect of, 42–44, 47,
    48–49
  economic man and, 49–50
  family-ancestral genes and, 38
  health variations, effect of, 41, 42
  held in common (HIC) genes and, 39
  life expectancy, effect on, 45–46
  not held in common (NHIC) genes and,
    39–40

  R criterion, 39
  reciprocity theory of, 46–48, 49
  selfish-gene theory and, 35–37
  wealth variations, effect of, 41–42
Anthropology, 167

Becker, G. S., 167
Berle, A. A., 121, 142, 144, 165–166
Biofuels, 27
Biological closeness, 42–44, 47, 48–49
Biology
  competition and, 169–172, 174
  equilibrium and, 167
  human behavior and, 167–168
  monopolies and, 169–172
  natural selection (*See* Natural selection)
  normative approach to, 176
  speciation problem in, 172–173, 176, 177
Blockholders, 154–155, 158–159
Buchanan, James M., 168

Capitalism, late arrival of. *See* Late arrival
  of capitalism
Capone, Al, 33
Carnegie, Andrew, 32
Central contractors
  corporations, in, 145–146, 147
  firms, in, 145–146
  proprietorships, in, 146–147
Central planning
  capitalism, effect on development of,
    79–80
  failure of, 80–81
Childbearing, 53
Child labor, effect on family size, 59–60

Child labor laws, effect on family size, 60,
61
Civility, 17
Civil service, 137
Closed corporations, 149
Coase, Ronald H.
efficient allocation of resources, on,
108–109, 110–114
FCC, on, 83–84
firms, on, 114–115, 121–122, 123, 127
identity of owner, on, 90, 100, 106
interdisciplinary approach and, 162
make-or-buy decision, on, 113
price system, on, 126
private ownership and, 90, 166
regulation, on, 117
transaction cost, on, 84, 106–107, 124
zero cost externalities, on, 100–102,
104–105
Coca-Cola, 137
Collectivism
primitive man and, 68
private ownership emerging from, 84
specialization, incompatibility with,
77–78
Commonality, interdisciplinary approach
and, 161–162, 168–169, 173–174
Communal rights, 97
Competition
biology and, 169–172, 174
decentralization distinguished, 175
normative approach to, 176
price system and, 175
status competition (*See* Status
competition)
Concern for others, relevance of, 9,
13–14
Content of private ownership, 95–100
Contract law, 17, 72
Contributions to causes, 14
Cooperation, 52–53
Coordination problem, 173
Corporations, 141–159
agency problems, 156
central contractors, 145–146, 147
closed corporations, 149
competition, protective nature of,
156–157
control of, 151–159
corporate model of firms, 121, 129

delegation of control to professional
management, 151–152
directors, 144–145
governance problems, 155–156
hostile takeovers, 156
insider trading, 155
institutional investors, advice for, 156
management of, 142–143
natural state of, 147–148
neoclassical theory, in, 165–166
overview, 143
ownership of, 143–151
partnerships contrasted, 149–150
personhood of, 141–142
proprietorships contrasted, 150
raising of capital by, 155
reasons for investing in, 155
regulation of, 157
shareholders (*See* Shareholders)
"shirking" in, 145–146
Smith on, 152–153
socialist firm compared, 141
social welfare policies, impact of,
157–158
stakeholder view of, 143–145
taxation of, 157
wealth distribution, impact of, 157–158
Costs of reciprocity, 47–48

Daley, Richard, 138
Darwin, Charles, 54, 161, 167, 172
Dawkins, Richard. *See also* Selfish-gene
theory
altered genes, on, 43–44
biological closeness, on, 47, 48–49
common ancestry, on, 42–43
decision-making process in selfish-gene
theory, 40–41
family-ancestral genes, on, 38, 39
gene *versus* person, 36, 37, 45
held in common (HIC) genes, on, 39
mechanism for selfish-gene theory,
44–45
not held in common (NHIC) genes, on,
39, 41
overview of selfish-gene theory, 34–36
Decentralization
competition distinguished, 175
coordination problem in, 173
industrialization and, 77–78

Index

Printed in the United States
By Bookmasters